# The Greatest Comeback

## Dr. Darryl Wheat

*First printed in 2019 in the United States of America by*

*ISBN: 978-1-953912-58-9*

*Library of Congress Catalog Card Number: 2020933453*

# What People are saying about "The Greatest Comeback."

## This book is a shining diamond.

UNBREAKABLE! A boy, then young man, now a man, who decidedly, relentlessly refused to let any person, any circumstance, or any criminal or legal system break him, his spirit, his sense of humor, and, more importantly, his sense of humanity. Proof positive it takes only one person, with heart, to support and guide an individual toward healthy options and survival. Each chapter is absolutely unpredictable! The author's wit, defiance, and courage are not lost on this reader who appreciated his ability to courageously and relentlessly hold a mirror up to the guards, cruel police officers and other adults in position of power to effectively reflect, in perfect form, the absurdity, the reality, the ridiculous cruelty that he and the other children faced in reform school; and of course, the abuse and violent situations he was forced to endure (for years) outside these children's prisons. **'WHY IS THIS NOT A MOVIE?' WAS MY THOUGHT ONLY A THIRD OF THE WAY THROUGH THIS BOOK.**

The shocking events that he and his grandmother shared will force me to reread this book and share it with anyone and everyone I can. This book should be on the reading list in college courses that have criminal justice, criminology, social work, sociology, counseling, and psychology.

The author went through hell and came out of it on his own terms—with dignity and sanity—as bright as a shining diamond. **BRILLIANT! WOW, WHAT A READ!**

J.P. Capps
Bachelor of Social Work
Graduate Student of Criminal Justice Administration and Forensic Psychology

## Read this shocking and powerful book.

Dr. Wheat's book is nothing short of intense, emotional, inspiring, breathtaking and brilliant. All parents of problem children, of families who have conflicts, will be inspired by this book. The author and his mentor (Nanny) bring us to this point: Either hate yourself and destroy yourself or change and learn to love your life. This book will never die. Both parents and professionals will be emotionally moved by this book. It will be a psychological classic. Read this great book.

C. Paul Smith, L.C.S.W.
Substance Abuse Disorder Specialist
G.V. (Sonny) Montgomery V.A. Medical Center
Jackson, Mississippi

## Incredibly Inspiring

Read this incredibly inspiring book. This book is a story about a person who faced severe obstacles, dramatic losses (parents), and from childhood to adulthood all the cards were stacked against you. This amazing story shows how the author bonded with one human being (his grandmother) and learned to believe in himself, believe in his dreams, and never give up. From age 5 to 19, life was a nightmare. He, with his grandmother's help, changed his life. You must read the last few chapters of this book. Great book, great author, great grandmother (Nanny.)

Chris Lancaster, L.C.S.W.
Trace Regional Hospital
Therapist
Houston, Mississippi

## A fabulous book!

A fabulous book! It should be a movie for all to see. I loved it. It captures your mind and your heart, and it teaches us the value of being loved, if only by one person. Abandoned by parents, kicked out of school, jailed dozens of times—his grandmother "Nanny" supports him until he succeeds. **HIS SUCCESSES ARE NO ORDINARY SUCCESSES. THEY ARE, IN FACT, MIRACULOUS.**

Christie Ross, L.C.S.W.
Clinical Social Worker
Madison, Mississippi

## This book is truly a masterpiece.

Dr. Wheat, this book is truly a masterpiece. His grandmother (Nanny) gave support to the fact that children today need structure, discipline, support, and unconditional love. The book is powerful and dramatic. His grandmother worked with him from age 5 to 19. From the abandonment of parents, reform school and jails, and through hundreds of unbelievable obstacles, his grandmother never gave up. Her relentless quest to help him was unconditional.

He not only survived; he becomes determined to accomplish the impossible. Read for yourself. His history is legendary.

Connie Jones, Attorney at Law
Public Defender, Rankin County Youth Court
Rankin County, Mississippi

## A Professional Classic and Should be a Movie

This book will be a professional classic and a movie for all to see. The book is brilliant. It will also break your heart, and then, in the end, lift you to heaven. Dr. Wheat is currently considered to be one of the most brilliant therapists in the South.

I began reading Dr. Wheat's book at a professional workshop I was attending, thinking it would just be another psychological book regarding foster children. On page 2, tears came to my eyes as I was reading, and I had to put the book down. After the workshop I picked up the book and read it in a few hours. The lessons that he and Nanny taught me are lifelong and paramount to anything I've ever read. Dr. Wheat fought for his sanity through chaos, trauma, rejection; however, his true savior was definitely his grandmother, Nanny. As I set the book down it showed me, as an adoptive mother, to keep attaching the kids I had adopted, show them love through their storms and their struggles and believe in the impossible.

Amy Cobb, Ph.D., LPC
Executive Director of Behavioral Health
United Healthcare
Jackson, Mississippi

## This is a great book. This book is even greater because it is a true story.

This is a true story. This is a great book! It's incredibly honest and a poignant account of the negative impact on children and their incarceration, whether detention, reform school, jails. How could any child survive the treatment that was imposed? The book creates indignation and is sad for obvious reasons. The atrocities that were committed by the Department of Corrections, police, and even the child's caretakers were horribly negative and almost impossible to overcome. All committed by people who were supposed to care for children. All of the rehabilitative training that was to be used for children was never instituted. Sometimes it was hard for me to even turn the page and read about a book full of consistent, unbelievable atrocities. What these children endured was sadistic, despite the rehabilitation that was promised. By reading this book, I can honestly say I learned as much from Nanny as Dr. Wheat. He had the help of an angel. In order to understand the beginning and the middle, one needs to read the ending. In my life-time, I have seen very few endings such as this. Great book!

Joyce Jackson, R.N.
Nurse Supervisor (Retired)
Meridian, Mississippi

## Read this great book!

When Bill Gates, the founder of Microsoft, was asked for a word of advice, he encouraged people to read. **In the same manner, I would encourage you to read Dr. Wheat's book.** He provides the readers with a tremendous and unforgettable asset on how to overcome adversity. As Executive Director of the Napoleon Hill Foundation, **I urge you to read this great book!**

Don Greene, Executive Director
Napoleon Hill Foundation
Wise, Virginia

To My Family - Momma, Janie, Laurie, Kerri, Jyn

∽

To Nanny
My first metaphysical teacher –
my beloved grandmother (Irma Slocum)
who began sharing her incredible wisdom
with me at age 5

∽

Special thanks to Amy Lofton, T.S. Koelling
and Steve Wilson

And
To all the boys who never stopped pushing me to write
this book

∽

To My Mentors:
Catherine Ponder, Joseph Murphy, Roy Eugene Davis,
William Ward, Robert Collier, Orison Marden, and
Napoleon Hill

∽

To Infinite Intelligence
for giving us the Power within

# Before you begin...

I had a definite purpose for writing this book. I want to teach and convince kids in trouble, kids rejected and neglected by parents, kids who live in the streets, and kids incarcerated and/or abused by their parents or other adults that they can change and still have a great life. That goes for adults as well.

I wanted to write a book that shows that people can change and become the person they want to be; that they can achieve their dreams and the things that people call *impossible*; that with struggle, sacrifice, persistence, and a *never-give-up attitude* they can change, reinvent their life, and live any great life they have imagined.

Anyone and everyone can get on a positive path and make the world a greater place.

# Table Of Content

Age: 18
Location: Alabama

## This had turned serious...

"Wheat…Wheat…WHEAT…**WHEAT! Cell door!**" demanded the captain of the jail.

The bunk creaked as I rolled over slowly from the cinder block wall to focus on the cell boss behind the man yelling. He opened his hands like, *I don't know what's going on.*

"What for?" I answered, focusing back on the man who was demanding my attention.

The yelling had awakened almost everyone in the cell block who was now curious to see what was going on. It certainly wasn't what normally happened at 5:00 a.m. at the jail.

The captain of the small Alabama jail, the place that had been my residence for the last four or five months, yelled, "Get all your stuff and bring it with you."

*Wow! Now what?* I stuffed my few belongings into the small bag that was with me when I first came to this tiny living space. I had never been issued a prison uniform, even though I had asked for one as I kept trying to clean the one set of clothes that I had worn when I was put here months ago. A shirt, socks, a toothbrush, a hat—not much to pack.

The captain repeated, emphatically this time, "**I said come to the cell door. Now!**"

"What are you doing to Little Wheat?" boomed a voice from somewhere across the way, another prisoner.

"None of your damn business!" was the response to the anonymous questioner.

As I stepped outside of the cell door, I was immediately attended to by two sheriff deputies. Two chains were wrapped around my stomach, with handcuffs attached that were snapped tightly on my wrists. Braces were clamped on each of my legs with a heavy chain between them linking them together. I asked the captain why I was being so bound, and where was I going with all these chains.

"Your chart says that you've been charged with 12 institutional escapes."

"That's not true," I snapped. "Most of them were just attempted escapes and not all of them were successful!"

"Just shut up, smart ass, and stand here!" the captain responded.

So that's what I did. Nervous. Off-balance. Paranoid. Suspicious. *Grateful, it was 5:30 in the morning*! The charges that they had interrogated me for up to this point ranged from kidnapping to car theft, attempted forgery, resisting arrest. I understood I was to be extradited to Fort Worth, Texas, but that hadn't happened yet. Instead, my time in this small cell had lasted from winter, where a bedsheet was the only source of warmth made available to the prisoners, due to the sweltering 100-degree weather that still continued. We felt each fluctuating degree in that place.

But the heat and cold weren't the only challenges. Other survival techniques had been learned quickly out of necessity—to survive these surroundings you had to establish your position with the other prisoners. Fast. My weight had dropped 30 pounds during my few months-long stay, and that was even after I had taken food from newcomers (forcefully) who came on the cell block. You could just about starve to death in this small-town jail.

All chains and locks were secured and checked. The captain, now satisfied, ordered, "Start walking. I want you to walk down those steps and out the right-hand side door."

"Where am I going?"

"Wherever I tell you to go!" was the only response I received.

I looked at him and said, "Well, that's great! Are you taking me on a fishing trip? Just the two of us together?"

The captain came back quickly. "I guess you being a smart ass is about to come to an end. How old are you now? Aren't you about 18 years old?"

"Yeah, I am. When I got here I was 17, but I'm 18 now." But I still wanted an answer. "Where am I going?"

"You're going to court," he said in a very cheerful voice.

My heart skipped a beat. *What, I'm going to court? I'm going to court? Are they serious? I'm going to court at 5:30 in the morning in a small Alabama town, from a small Alabama jail, with chains on my legs, chains around my waist, handcuffed, with a small bag of every-thing that I own; and I'm going to court. Oh, my God! The United States and state of Alabama court, at 5:30 in the morning!*

*Nobody in America has court at 5:30 in the morning!*

We left the jail and proceeded towards the courthouse, about a 50-yard walk, with the leg chains being of no help. I'm thinking to myself, *Has this local jail gotten fed up with me? And since Fort Worth has not proceeded with extradition, is Alabama going to press some charge or charges against me and sentence me to their jail? Or even Rayford State Penitentiary?*

The court house was completely lit up at 5:30 in the morning. Apparently, my arrival had been anticipated. I walked up the steps. Once inside the main door, the captain kept pushing me in the back, down the hall and into an actual courtroom. I was beginning to feel a deep sense of anxiety. I was tense and felt helpless. *An actual court hearing at 5:30 in the morning? This is beyond strange! It just doesn't happen! Something strange is going to happen!*

A place for me to sit was indicated. It was just about six feet in front of the judge, who I now faced. He looked to be between 40 and 50, had the face of a younger man but, like all judges, seemed very serious. He was dressed in all black, which was an indication that some judgment was going to happen. *They sure are making it look like the real thing!*

The judge broke the silence. "In just a minute we're going to proceed with your court hearing."

My understanding of courtroom protocol was that a bailiff was usually in attendance but a glance around the room dismissed the idea that anyone but the three of us were present.

Again, the judge spoke. "Darryl Wheat, correct?"
"Yes, Your Honor."

The judge was now demanding my full attention. "Mr. Darryl Wheat, for your information, we have been sent your voluminous criminal record from Louisiana. You have been here an extended length of time. How many…uh, five or six months, I think, waiting for extradition. We have come to some conclusions which are going to be resolved this morning."

I said nothing. I just sat there. *There's an explosion coming!*

The judge looked past me and raised his voice. "Henry! Henry!"

A big, tall, muscular black male, very friendly, very polite, responded to the summons. Apparently, this was Henry. Henry was given instructions by the judge to find the other members of the early-morning courthouse cleaning staff, Maria and her daughter, and to bring them with him into the courtroom. Henry left the room and shortly reappeared in the doorway with the others in tow. It was obvious from their body language that they were clueless as to what was going on and remained at the door waiting for the judge to direct them.

"Henry, Maria, you and your daughter sit in the jurors' section. Henry, you are head of the jury. You are the captain. You are going to consult with the other two people in the jury, and that's Maria and her daughter. Do you understand?"

A confused Henry answered, "Yes, sir."

"Have a seat, Henry."

The judge's attention snapped back to me. "Mr. Darryl Wheat, come and stand in front of me before the court." Chains and all, I shuffled to the indicated spot. "Mr. Wheat, I would like to speak with you. Mr. Wheat, you have been a problem in our jail for about five or six months. You have exhibited complete defiance, negative verbal comments, a lack of cooperation, and apparently a lack of fear of what the law can do to you. I see from your record that you have served time in many places and jails for many different reasons. You have been in jail, detention halls, and juvenile centers across any number of different cities in Louisiana—New Orleans, Alexandria, Baton Rouge, Monroe, New Roads, Port Allen, and also your record reflects time in reform school. And now you've been held in our Alabama jail. Much of your teenage life has been in the streets, not in school. And your charges range from aggravated assault, car theft, burglary of a train depot, which sounds like a federal offense to me, and from what I understand serious aggravated battery charges by the dozens. I assume this means fistfights. Also, assaulting a schoolteacher, being expelled from school 10 to 15 times, incarcerated in a reformatory in Louisiana, and three parole violations and correctional jail escapes. I could go on and on and on, couldn't I? There are many more pages here. Correct?"

"Is that a question, Your Honor?" I'm a little incredulous at this point. "I'm not looking at the file you're holding. I don't know, Your Honor. I didn't write all that. All the things you're holding were written by other people."

The judge looked at me, put his hand on his forehead and leaned back, shaking his head from side to side. "I have two things that I want to happen today. Henry, you're going to find Mr. Wheat not guilty for any of the charges we have interrogated him for. Do you understand?"

"Yes sir," Henry responded quickly.

"You are to write it down on the tablet that's on the stand and hand it to me," said the judge. "Mr. Wheat, you're going to plead not guilty. Then I'm going to find you not guilty. Then you're going to have one hour to contact someone who might be able to wire you some money to get out of this town. Or, you may hitchhike out of this town. Or, you may walk or you may run out of this town. But you are never, never, never to come back to my town again. Do you understand?"

I was stunned about what I was hearing, so I asked, "Did you say I'm supposed to plead not guilty?"

"That's what I said."

"So," I said, "okay. I plead not guilty."

The judge shifted his attention back to the papers in front of him. "We will now proceed with what you've been charged with. The charges right now that are from Fort Worth, Alabama, Georgia and Baton Rouge, Louisiana have been neutralized to some extent because, even though you crossed state lines, under Alabama law you are legally married. Under these new conditions, you basically would only be charged with auto theft. You claim that you did not know it was a stolen car. Still, you crossed all three state lines in what was a stolen car. I don't know what the other states are going to do and I don't care. Your accomplice says he's willing to buy the car and the charges have been dropped in Baton Rouge, Louisiana.

"Also, I could mention that you've attempted to undo the jail commode in our jail piece by piece, brick by brick in an attempt to escape for the thirteenth time, so the jailors tell me. These charges are not going to be brought forth by this court, neither will your constant resistance of arrest and lack of cooperation. Your original lying about your history, assaults, and fistfights occurring within the jail during your visit here are not going to be dealt with by this court. Now, let me tell you what is going to be dealt with by this court today. Right now.

"You are going to be found not guilty of any charges. There is no way of convicting you in this circumstance. Do you understand that, Mr. Wheat? I think this file, which we received from Louisiana, covers just about as much delinquency as I have seen in my judicial career. I've known many young people who have committed crimes but it looks to me like you have been arrested dozens of times." The judge's facial expression was now serious. "Nevertheless, Mr. Wheat, do you plead guilty or not guilty?"

It was my turn. "Not guilty, Your Honor."

The scratching of a pen on the judge's desk indicated that he had signed the document and the proceeding had concluded and was being made official. Henry walked hesitantly from the jury box and handed the judge a piece of paper as he had been instructed.

Settling back into his chair, the man in the black robe was ready to make his final declaration. "In that case, Mr. Wheat, you are hereby acquitted of all charges and they have been dropped. You are free to leave this court. Captain, take the handcuffs and leggings off of Mr. Wheat at this time."

At this point, I was confused. "What am I supposed to do?" I asked the judge.

The judge answered, speaking slowly and emphatically. "It's easy. You are to leave here as fast as you are capable of doing so, before the State of Alabama finds something else, or one of these police officers at our jail finds a way to press charges for any of the absolutely defiant behaviors you've committed while incarcerated here. Anyway, you have approximately one hour and a half to complete calling whoever you call that may send you some money to get out of here, or to walk out of here or to run out of here, but you are to leave this city and my county."

Acknowledging the presence of the captain for the first time, the judge voiced a plan of action. "There is a city limit sign, officer. Will you take him to the city limit sign and drop him off?" The captain gave a slight nod in the affirmative.

Redirecting his focus back to me, "I would like for you to leave the state of Alabama as soon as you can, Mr. Wheat. Do you understand?"

"Yes, sir. I understand perfectly."

The captain approached me, talking to the judge, "We ought to leave these handcuffs on until I let him go on the other side of the city limits."

The judge repeated, looking at him, "No. I said no charges. Take them off."

My gaze shifted from the judge's face to settle on the captain's.

"You'd like that, wouldn't you? You get a kick out of your job, don't you?" The captain came back with, "You're not out of here yet, smartass."

Silence prevailed in the courtroom except for the chains being rattled as keys were turned in the locks to remove the confinements that had been so over-the-top from the beginning.

Mother received the only call I was allowed. She sent $20 through Western Union and I told her I'd explain later.

I was put in the captain's car and ordered to sit in the back seat. I had — $20 in my pocket and the captain was supposed to take me to the city limits. The plan came to an abrupt halt when the captain pulled over on the side of the road about forty yards short of the sign and told me to get out of the car.

*This is not what the judge had instructed! The captain has come up with a new game plan!* "I thought you were going to take me to the city limits?"

"You thought wrong, that's what you thought." The captain had slid out of the car and was holding my door open. His hand remained close to the gun still holstered. "You've caused me more trouble in the time that you've been here than in all of my fifty years as a police officer. And because you're such a smart ass, I want to show you something."

The holster flap was released quickly and the gun slipped smoothly from where it had rested. He cocked his gun and said, "Now, take off running."

"Excuse me?"

The volume the second time around was slightly increased. "I said, 'take off running.'"

My attitude had not been left behind in the courtroom. "Or if I don't take off running, then what?"

He said, "You'll find out. Your hour is up and you're supposed to be on the other side of that sign."

Instead, I deliberately started walking. *This was getting scary!* He started putting bullets into his gun. I started running and dove into a ditch as a bullet passed over the top of my head. The ditch was wet from morning dew. Another shot streaked over my head and hit a barbed wire fence about fifteen feet in front of me. I made a low run for the fence and crawled under it. There was morning wet all over me.

The sun was coming up now. There was a tree about twenty yards from me that became my next goal. I tried to crawl to the tree and put my back against it, but three shots rang out and bark flew everywhere. *That makes five!* My assumption was that he had a six-chamber gun. I pushed on in a direction away from the source of the gun blasts but another shot rang out, this time hitting the city limit sign and putting a hole in it.

I kept crawling through the grass and trees, way past the city limit sign, but I didn't hear any more shots.

Eventually, I hoisted myself into a low, crouching run for probably about half a mile through a wooded area without hearing anyone following me. But I wouldn't have put it past the captain to still be back there.

I emerged from the woods about a half-mile down the road and started walking. I didn't know which direction I was headed, but I was wet and I was tired and my wrists were killing me from where the handcuffs had dug in. I thumbed a ride from a truck driver who took me to the main highway where we parted ways. The $20 in my pocket wasn't going to get me very far but I had to figure out how to get back to Baton Rouge. The sun was high, the road was hot and my feet were tired, my clothes were wet, but finally, a car headed in the right direction stopped and gave me a ride.

A lot had happened in the span of a two-hour time-frame, and a lot had changed. I woke up this morning looking at my world through a set of vertical bars. The bars were no longer in front of me, but now I had to figure not only how to get home, but also how to get me back to Nanny. The trip was harder than I thought it would be…

Age: 5
Location: Baton
Rouge, Louisiana

2

# Maybe I should start at the beginning...

My mother and father were discussing something in the kitchen of the house where we lived in the Bellfair section of Baton Rouge, Louisiana. I had lived in Baton Rouge all my life.

Mother was drinking her Coca Cola in the kitchen and had set it down on the counter. Mother was pregnant. In the evenings I sat on the porch swing with her and would put my hand on her stomach. I could feel my sister thumping. My father seemed to be indifferent to her pregnancy. He just stated he hoped it was a boy.

My father was very controlling, very aggressive, and a very tough person. He was handsome but had a terrible temper. Even his own brothers were afraid of him.

Anyway, my mother and father were in the kitchen and for some reason, he hit her in the face. He reached over and took the Coke bottle and hit her with it. She fell to the floor. He started ripping her clothes as she lay on the floor. He thought she was lying about where she had been. I think that she had taken me out to Louisiana State University that day for my appointment. That's where people were "studying me" because I was able to read at two-and-a-half years of age. I could read adult books at age three, which at that time nobody thought was possible.

They were actually studying me at University High School on the campus of LSU. Teachers or researchers would come and ask me to read or write certain passages out of books and ask me questions.

Anyway, back to the scene between my mother and father. I ran and grabbed my father around the neck and he swung me across the room. I hit the wall and was able to get up to run back to him and put my arms around his neck again. He threw me across the room again. He left my mother to get up by herself but he had really hurt her bad. He went outside and sat on the back steps. Mother quickly gathered some clothes together for me and for the soon-to-be baby and then took the baby's stroller and rolled it to the street. We were going to walk to my grandmother's house.

I walked across the property to the back to join my mother. My father yelled at me to come and kiss him goodbye.

I told him, "No."

He said, "I said come kiss me goodbye."

I walked across the backyard where he was sitting on the steps and kicked him in the shins. He picked me up, took me to the garage, locked the door where my mother couldn't get to me, and beat me with a piece of wood for what seemed like 15 to 20 minutes. He hit me with a board until I finally lost consciousness. At some point, he opened the garage door and my mother came in and took me by the hand to go with her. What I remember most was my decision that no one would ever hit me with a board again. Ever.

Mother and I started walking to my grandmother's house. She had a black eye and the side of her face was turning black where he had hit her. Blood was coming out of the top of my eye and my mouth, and some of the bruises where he had hit me were already starting to turn blue.

Nanny's house was about a mile away. We walked and we were going to a place that would become very important to my existence. We walked all the way to my grandparents' house—to my Nanny's house.

I was about five-and-a-half years old when all of this happened. Nanny took me under her wing immediately. She talked to me extensively and asked me questions every morning after I got there. It seems that shortly after we arrived Mother would take a bus downtown to business school each morning. I never saw her during the daytime. The days were spent with Nanny.

During that time of my life, every single morning I had coffee and breakfast with Nanny. Each day we talked about something new. She would ask me questions. She complimented my reading. She would ask me to read to her and then ask me what it meant. For some neurological or biological reason, I was able to read adult books at the age of three and would come across concepts that I didn't understand and she would tell me some part of what they meant in a more simple form. We did this every morning. My grandfather felt comfortable with our daily routine.

*"Read, read, read. Listen to the great dreamers and achievers. Their teachings can help you understand universal truth and experience miracles and, of course, connect with infinite intelligence."*
**Nanny**

My sister was born sometime after I started school and the three of us called this our home. We lived there and I attended elementary school in the first grade at Fairfields Elementary on Fairfields Drive in Old Fairfields, a subdivision off of Plank Road. But before I attended school, I asked my grandmother to talk to my mother about the daily trips to be studied by the teachers and researchers at LSU. I felt lonely because people would ask me questions, and then repeatedly keep leaving the room to discuss my responses, leaving me alone and afraid. My mother would stay out in the hall so I couldn't talk to her and I didn't even know where she was. I didn't like it and I asked my grandmother to talk to my mother and end this going out to LSU. All of this occurred before going to the first grade.

I remember going out to LSU, but I was actually going to some high school next door called University High School, which was apparently on the campus of LSU. I don't know what they were looking for other than the fact that the whole thing centered around some amazement that I could read, learn, and explain what I was reading at two-and-a-half years old. At five years old, at my grandmother's house, I had my own library. I think they found that unusual and strange and used words like brilliant, genius, and things such as that. I didn't know what they were talking about. It had no meaning for me. I just wanted to quit. They certainly told my mother they had never seen a child like me before and while it seemed natural to me, apparently it wasn't to everyone else.

We remained living with my grandmother during the time that I attended school. Several boys in the neighborhood picked on my little sister and my grandfather asked me if I was going to protect her. At that point in time, I went out with a cap pistol and hit each one of them in the head. Some required stitches in the emergency room. I remember that seemed to be the beginning of my tendency toward fighting. The parents in the subdivision didn't particularly like it and would call my mother, who would then tell me how I was supposed to act. My grandfather disagreed with her, and approved of me being aggressive and protecting myself and my sister. Presumably, I fought well because I quickly gained a reputation in my neighborhood that I should be left alone.

Age: 7 or 8
Location: Baton Rouge,
Louisiana

**3**

# Her choice did not include me...

When I was about seven or eight years old, Mother met a man. He temporarily moved into Nanny's house with her. They got married and he and I didn't get along from the very beginning. He didn't like me, and when my grandparents weren't around, he was mean and critical. They bought a house about a mile from Nanny's house. The day that he and my mother and sister packed to leave and move into their new house, I packed my small suitcase that had been a gift from Nanny and we all went out on the front lawn to leave. As everyone was piling into the car to leave, I remember my mother leaning out the window and asking my grandmother, "Didn't you tell him?"

For a moment, I was confused. My grandmother looked at my mother seriously and stated slowly, "No, that is your job."

Mother said, "Oh." Mother then shifted her attention to me. "You're staying here and you're going to live with your grandmother."

Up until that moment, my mother and I had been completely and totally united. My mother was protective, compassionate, sensitive, affectionate, and had been teaching and standing next to me all of my life. My mind began changing the moment she said it. Unbelievably, her husband started the car, and they drove off. They drove off, and I just stood there with my suitcase in my hand in utter and total disbelief. There had been no communication between Mother and me, no warning, no comforting. The surprise was like an explosion. Her statement came across the airwaves like an atomic bomb. I felt emotionally paralyzed and devastated beyond belief.

I stood by the curb for a long time thinking a mistake had been made and I would see the car coming back again in my direction. It didn't. Finally, I walked around and went inside Nanny's house. I put my suitcase on the bed, got behind the bed that I had been sleeping in since we had moved in, and gripped the bedspread and sheets with both hands. I was trying to hold on to something tangible as well as trying to hold onto my mind. I stayed behind the bed the rest of the day. At some point, my grandmother came in and set some food on the floor near me and left. I must have gone to sleep and spent the night behind the bed, because that's where I found myself the next morning. When I woke up, I found Nanny on the back porch. Nobody was there except the two of us. I remember that conversation and it was an emotional interaction. She talked. I did most of the listening. Apparently, I didn't go to school that day. I was still stunned by the experience. It felt like a bad dream. It was like a psychological tsunami. I was in a state of pain, extreme loss, shock, and was finding it hard to integrate my mother driving off and leaving me. I was unable to soothe myself and I was seriously devastated.

I can say that my mind and my life changed at that moment. Strangely, my grandmother seemed to be totally in tune with what I was feeling. I remember the conversation on the back porch. I would never forget it. Calmly and quietly she talked to me. Nanny was always straightforward. She never talked to you like a child. She always used adult conversation and could be brutally honest. I guess this was the beginning of a great and complex relationship that I would never forget. She stated she had had four children, but this situation made her feel like I was the fifth child. The conversation consisted of asking me to think about things or try to understand things. She told me she was going to do things for me and with me that she had not even done with her other four children. I might add that her other four children, which included my mother, were very smart, very well educated, and highly respected in the community.

> *"I would rather see you Stand Tall in Life…than become less than what you can be.*
> *Overcome your obstacles, don't join them. Be courageous.*
> *I'm behind you."*
>
> **Nanny**

Anyway, she stated, "I will be behind you no matter what, and I mean no matter what. Do you understand what I'm saying?"

I said, "Yes, I understand."

She said, "Tell me what I just said."

And I repeated, "You will stand behind me no matter what."

She held my chin up and looked into my eyes. Nanny was very deep, brilliant, serious, and very tough. She was always serious and she meant what she said. She was powerful, strong, articulate, incredibly independent, and attached to the truth by the hip. She was five foot six, stood tall, medium boned, afraid of no one or any circumstance, was never pushed around by anybody in the neighborhood or politics or business.

She reemphasized a comment that took me all of my youth to understand. She said, "I told you I would stand behind you no matter what, and I mean what I'm saying."

There were several things I didn't understand that day. I didn't know how damaged I was by my mother's abandonment. I also didn't realize how much effort my grandmother was willing to put in to raising me as her "fifth child." But I certainly had no idea how much I would come to depend on Nanny's statement, "I told you I would stand behind you no matter what, and I mean what I'm saying."

Age: 5 through 7th grade
Location: Baton Rouge,
Louisiana

# My life was getting ready to drastically change...

Iarrived at my grandmother's house at approximately age 5. I could not have known how this would impact my life and influence the person I would eventually become, or that I would come to view this as a place of comfort and strength. Nanny became the center of my life. Every morning Nanny and I had coffee and breakfast as a routine. I mean, sincerely, every single morning.

One of the first things that happened was that she called me out to the back porch and said she wanted to show me two different things. I loved baseball and always had some kind of ball in my hand. She asked me for the ball.

She said, "I have the ball in my hand and I want you to watch what I do"

And I said, "Okay."

She took the ball, held it about waist high and dropped it. She said, "You saw the ball in my hand and you saw the ball hit the floor. Okay. Did you see anything between the ball and it hitting the floor?"

I said, "No, nothing."

She said, "All that you didn't see is there and all that you didn't see is invisible and all that you didn't see will make everything that you want in life possible. I know that you don't understand at this time but I'm going to teach you."

I said, "Okay." I wasn't sure what she meant but her intensity and lovingness and seriousness came across strongly. I learned quickly to believe and trust Nanny. Nanny had a sense of humor but, when she was being serious, she always stated the truth. She had stated that whether the truth was painful or whether the truth might make you happy, people needed to know the truth, needed to understand and live with the truth.

Anyway, to go on, she said, "I'm going to help you understand people." And I said, "Okay."

And she said, "I'm going to teach you a lot about living as we go along. I'm going to help you understand your own feelings as well. Don't worry, we're going to take this one step at a time." She said, "Each morning we're going to talk about a topic or something that you've read or that I've read, or you saw or that you want to know, and we will discuss it and talk about it with each other."

I said, "All right."

She then explained about the ball. She said, "When I dropped the ball and it hit the floor what you can't see is the invisible and there's a lot there between the ball and it hitting the floor. I'm going to teach you about that as life goes by. Understanding the invisible can help you make great changes in your life. Other people sometimes call these changes miracles. You believe something you can't see and you act as if it's there, and then you will be able to see it. It doesn't matter what we call what we can't see. It can go by different names. We can call what we can't see God, spirit, divine intelligence, infinite intelligence, or universal mind. It really doesn't matter. But I'm going to teach you about what you can't see in between me letting the ball go from my hand and the ball hitting the floor."

Nanny didn't stop there. She went into the kitchen, filled a glass half full, and brought it back to the back porch. And she said, "You see that the glass is half full of water and that the other half of the glass has no water?" And she said, "You see the water. You can put your finger in it, correct?"

I said, "Yes."

She said, "That's called substance."

She said, "The other half of what's in the glass is invisible, isn't that correct? So you can see that half of the glass is invisible. What's invisible is a different kind of substance. That's what you're going to learn about life. Life is about two things—what's

> "If you believe in miracles, you will experience them."
> **Nanny**

at the bottom and what's invisible. I know that's pretty complicated right now, but that's okay. This is where we're going to start our teaching. How long it takes is less important than for you to finally understand it. If I were to leave you tomorrow, those two things that I have just taught you are the most important things you will ever need to know."

To the best of my memory, I will quote some of the things she taught me over the weeks, months, and years...

* "Everything is possible. Those people that can see the invisible can do the impossible."

* "If I'm not around, or if you're in a bad or scary circumstance, or if anything should happen to me, read the 91st Psalm and take it literally just like it says."

* "Remember that you may not understand the things I'm telling you right now, but little by little as life goes on, we always understand more. Just like you're able to read more and more, you're going to be able to understand more and more."

* "Life is full of abundance, and you're standing in diamonds. I know you don't know what that means, but you will."

* "You're standing at heaven's gate but you're the only one who can get you inside."

* "You're able to take ten times more pain than you think you can."

* "You can accomplish ten times more than you think you can."

* "Whatever you dream that you could accomplish, you're capable of making it real. All of your dreams can come true when you learn how to believe in yourself."

* "When you're trying to do something that seems hard, you never quit.

In life, you have to have 'bulldog' tenacity. You have to be tough."

* "What you can't see, and didn't see when I dropped the ball, can be used if you believe in it. If you have faith in the invisible you didn't see (God), then that source will lovingly help you. It promises help. All you have to do is ask."

* "You can have anything you want if you believe. Have faith. Visualize like a dream inside your mind. Give up some things you don't need in order to get greater things. Persist and never give up once you have decided what it is you want. And then, I know it sounds crazy, act like you have it already. And when those things come true, be thankful and show your gratitude and thankfulness."

* "Don't let people hurt you. Try to remember that you're going to hate what some people say or do. But try to remember that it's useless to hate them. It's best just to hate the way they act or the things that they do, but hating them is useless and unnecessary. You will find in

life that people are either weak or strong. You will have to learn in life how to become strong, very strong."

* "If you realize that there's something great inside of you…and although it is invisible, it is very powerful and always on your side, then it will always be a source of strength for you. You should not be fearful of this power; it is always there to benefit you.

At another time, she said, "You remember in the Bible when David faced the giant?"

I said, "Yes, ma'am."

She said, "David didn't fear the giant, did he?"

I said, "No."

She said, "The reason is there's no such thing as a giant, although it can look that way. Life is tough but you have to be tougher. There's no such thing as a giant. That is a fantasy. It's all in your mind. There's nothing you can't accomplish on your own and there's nothing that you can't have if you use your mind to believe, act, and have faith."

As time went on, every morning Nanny and I met and we talked about different topics. Each morning I would go to school and come back and sometimes we would talk a little more and sometimes not. I might say that while I spent six years in grammar school at Fairfields Elementary, I don't remember much about the academic part of it. I do remember that the school contacted my grandmother. She told me what they said, that I might do an assignment, that I might not. The teachers reported to

Nanny that I was extremely brilliant but wasn't necessarily cooperative with class assignments or seemed to show any anxiety about the consequences. The teachers also seemed to be perplexed about how polite and courteous I was to them and to students, but, if threatened by a student, I was quick to become angry and fight. Her response to them was, "Just try to work with him the best that you can. He gets bored very, very easily and it's not easy to get him to do something he doesn't want to do."

I recall bringing and reading during class literary works by Napoleon Hill, John Bunyan, Jack London, James Allen, and Orison Marden and works about Joan of Arc, Helen Keller, and George Fox, to name a few. Apparently, the teachers adapted to my behavior and seemed to be shocked or amazed and often counted my reading choices as a grade for their class.

Regardless of what happened in school, however, my grandmother and I still had coffee and breakfast every morning before I went to school. I remember that I had a few fights in school. I remember that she questioned me about why they happened, but wasn't surprised to have the teachers report this about me based on what she had already seen of my behavior. I think she had expected that I would take up for myself.

Of great importance was that at around 10 or 11 years old, I would typically spend my evenings throwing a tennis ball against the outside steps in the back of the house trying to emulate major league pitchers that I had heard on the radio. They were able to throw pitches described as curveballs, drops, sliders, et cetera. I loved baseball and I was obsessed with trying to learn how to throw those pitches. Later on, at the end of the sixth grade, I played American Legion baseball. I was the pitcher. The team was made up of kids from our subdivision, Fairfields, and Bellfair. Nanny's contribution was to remind me to focus and believe and persist. An important thing to mention is that my mother bought a very expensive baseball glove for me and paid for it fifty cents or one dollar at a time on a weekly basis. To this day, I still have that glove. The local drugstore, Middleton Drugs, sponsored us. In the sixth grade, we won the championship. It was highly unexpected and the newspaper and radio in Baton Rouge began to follow our team.

We came together as a great team and the following year, with me as the leading pitcher, we won 11 games, no losses, and I pitched eight no-hitters. I won the American Legion Trophy, which was the first time the award had ever been instituted. Middleton Drugs won the championship, and while I was standing on the mound after the game, Mr. Smiley, who was in charge of American Legion Baseball, announced they were going to recognize a Baseball Star of the Year. He brought out the baseball that had been used

> *"Demand success...be persistent, aim high, reach for the stars, and sit with God"*
>
> *Nanny*

in the final game, wrote his name on it and announced my achievements to a large crowd of people I hadn't even noticed. There must have been hundreds of people who stood up and clapped for me. I was surprised and shocked. It was a great feeling. I was so devoted and committed and intense about baseball that I hadn't paid much attention to the fact that more and more people were coming to see the games that I played in and that Middleton Drugs was winning. The results of these games began appearing in the Baton Rouge newspaper in the sports section. On one occasion, I even appeared on the "Buckskin Bill Show" showing and demonstrating how I threw certain pitches such as curveballs, drops, and sliders that apparently were supposed to be impossible for a person my age.

At that time I had gone from 12 to 13 and it was a great time in my life, even though my family didn't go to the games. Nanny would question me about the games when I would get home and she would be exceedingly proud of me. It's something you never forget. She asked me to see the baseball and she wrote on it, "Who will play on a great and bigger league someday." I still have the ball to this day.

As far as academics, the seventh grade school year wasn't much different from the fifth or sixth grade. They seemed to think their books and assignments were the greatest things since sliced bread, but I could finish reading them over the weekend. That went over like a lead balloon with the teachers. That obviously was not the path I was supposed to be taking or the way I was supposed to handle their assignments. The teachers were indifferent, more disciplinary, more corrective, less patient, and more sarcastic. I didn't like the way I was corrected, especially by male teachers, or the way I was treated.

Anyway, Nanny taught me many, many things about myself, about life, and about others from the first through the seventh grade but there were some drastic mental changes taking place in me. I was feeling more and more anger and indifference. Maybe I resented male correction but I also resented the way I was being corrected. Basically, you might say that I was attached to my grandmother and grandfather, the baseball team, my neighborhood, and a few friends. Baton Rouge Junior High seemed to be like a foreign country.

Age: 12 - 13, 8th grade
Location: Baton Rouge,
Louisiana

## As predicted, life changed fast...

I only survived the seventh grade because I played baseball during that year, but the eighth grade started off even worse. The courses and materials were not interesting or challenging, and I didn't see how I would ever use many of them in my adult life.

For example, I remember typing class. I couldn't type. Neither did I like typing. Finally, out of frustration, I threw the typewriter out of the second-story classroom window. The west side of Baton Rouge Junior High was covered with concrete, so the typewriter hit and pieces went everywhere. When the teacher found out that I was the one who did it, she calmly asked me to go pick up the pieces and bring them to her. She allowed me to read books that I brought from home every day for the rest of the year.

And then there were history and math classes, both of which could easily have been accomplished in a week or two instead of a full year. Again, I chose just to bring books from home, sign my name and put a zero at the top of the tests and pass them back in, as I did in typing.

I guess I became frustrated, indifferent to school, and certainly not in any mood to be picked on by other students. So, the result was more fighting and being more aggressive, which, oddly enough, attracted more people who wanted to challenge me. People who fight a lot gain a reputation, so, if you get into fights, it seems to develop into more fights. I didn't start any of the fights, but I wouldn't say I didn't hit somebody first, meaning if I knew they were going to fight me I might hit them first.

Most of the time, I would get a suspension from school, usually because I won the fight. The principal had originally wanted to give me paddle licks and send me back to class, which resulted in a rather heated conversation between the two of us, in which I let him know that I didn't take licks with a paddle…from anyone. After a number of suspensions, he changed his method of punishment to having me sit with him in the office and running errands for him. That was the first semester of the eighth grade.

During the second semester, I met several people who seemed to have a similar circumstance as mine. I think there was about five of us. And the second half of the eighth grade veered drastically off course after that.

In a way, I guess, I quit participating in school and instead brought personal books from home by authors that I liked, such as Thomas Wolfe, Ernest Hemingway, Fitz-

gerald, John Steinbeck, Emerson, Lord Byron, Dostoyevsky, and Thoreau. I loved Wolfe, Steinbeck, and Thoreau. These writers really meant something to me, and I
felt a kinship with them and a lot of their beliefs. At least
the ones I could understand. I found Emerson more difficult, for example, than Thoreau. I used the classroom for
sitting and reading. However, I can't say the same about
my sessions with Nanny each morning and sometimes
after school. We always discussed the thoughts, ideas,
comments, and sentences in the books I was reading.
This became a ritual for us every morning over breakfast
before I went to school. If I passed anything in the eighth
grade, it was not by my effort, and it was the school's
decision to promote me to the ninth grade.

There was no baseball that summer, so the people I
had met during that semester and I ran the streets. I had
no money to get around, so life became breaking into
businesses, getting into picture shows for free, and even
going into a local bar and getting people to buy alcohol
for me, which contributed to an increase in fighting.

On one occasion during the last part of the eighth
grade, I was by myself on the school grounds reading
one of my books during the student lunchtime when I
turned to the back page and saw a note from Nanny. She
had taped a quarter to the back of the book with a note
saying, "Today you can eat with the other students." It
struck me that that was a sacrifice for her. My grandparents were retired and they didn't have the money to

support me. I decided then and there, at the age of 13, that no more quarters from Nanny were going to be necessary; somehow I would get the money for whatever I needed.

Naturally, acquiring excess money would require either a part-time job or stealing. I started shoplifting and selling things to people my age or older. I even found out that you could steal certain things and the pawnshop would pay you for them. I remember being caught for stealing records and being given a three-month probationary sentence. It seemed easy. I went one time a week to talk to a probation officer and that was it. Big deal. Easy enough. My family didn't even find out about it. True story.

I continued to steal and shoplift, and on one occasion I remember I had to spend a couple of nights in the detention home, which in reality increased my skills regarding stealing—what to steal, what to sell it for, who to sell it to.

Naturally, living in the streets leads to trouble. I remember going over to Memorial Stadium (off Scenic Highway) just to think about life. There were already some boys there and there was also a small stream or creek that ran nearby. One of the boys, standing on the opposite side of the water from me, stated, "You're on the wrong side of the creek."

I said I wasn't.

He threatened me and said, "I think you need to leave." I told him I wasn't leaving to go anywhere.

He threatened me with a .22 rifle. He said, "I'll shoot you if you don't leave."

I said, "If you're going to do it, do it."

So he did it. While some bullets went by my face and arm, two hit me in the stomach. I took off to Nanny's house and she dug the bullets out, which were just barely under the skin. She used an ice pick, then iodine then sutured the areas with needle and thread, and used gauze and old-fashioned adhesive tape around my stomach. I started walking out away from home. She only asked one question…. "Do I need to ask where you're going?"

> *"Fear no one…it's the opposite of self-confidence."*
>
> **Nanny**

I said, "No, ma'am. I'll be back in a little while."

I went back to the creek and started roaming in the neighborhood streets. I recognized one of the boys who had been with the shooter and he quickly told me where the shooter lived. I found the house and kicked open the screen door, went down the hallway, and dove over the supper table at the boy and we fought. His mother heard us and came running into the kitchen. When she asked me what was going on, I said, "He shot me."

The mother pulled out a rolling pin from a nearby drawer and was going to hit her son with it. I caught her and said, "You can't hit him in the head. That's where his brain is. You're going to kill him."

She said, "I don't believe this. Are you being serious?" I said, "Yes, ma'am."

The fighting between us had stopped and she looked around the kitchen. She said to her son, "You clean up the kitchen." She then looked at me and asked, "Would you like to stay for supper?"

During supper, I learned her anger towards her son was due to his father being in the penitentiary and she was afraid that her son would soon be following his father there. Anyway, he and I became friends.

I guess I began being at the wrong places at the wrong times. I was stabbed in the back at a local fair for talking to a girl. I was so angry, I took the knife out of my shoulder, hit him several times and knocked him down and put the knife to his throat. This was probably in front of about 30 to 50 kids. We had an audience. My adrenaline was so high, it took everything I had to keep from cutting him. He looked terrified. I let him up, closed the knife, put it in his mouth and told him to get out of there and never come around me again. The adrenaline that had hit me was different and strong. I was finding myself more intense, experiencing more rage and aggression. I was less willing to put up with anyone's aggression or verbal threats; I was also more willing to hurt someone who was attempting to do so. I guess living in the streets does that to you.

I spent the majority of my daytime hours away from home sneaking into shows, stealing, riding around in someone else's car, but then I would always go home. My grandfather had a rule that if I came in after 12 he would leave a pillow and a blanket on the back porch. But usually I would unlock one of the windows before I left, sneak in, lock the window and go to bed and wake up to have breakfast with Nanny and, of course, our talks, the next morning.

That summer led to a very traumatic ninth-grade year at Baton Rouge Junior High School. However, how could it be anything but traumatic based on the destructive life choices I was already making?

Age: 13 - 14, Ninth grade
Location: Baton Rouge,
Louisiana

## My interest in attending the ninth grade was zero...

I registered for school in the ninth grade, but I think when they asked me about how to arrange my classes and my plan for the future I told them I actually didn't care, whatever they wanted to do. No books came home with me from school. I didn't study and I didn't make any pretense to my teachers or grandmother and grandfather that I was going to. From class tests to classwork to homework, I participated in almost nothing that was associated with school. Tests that were on the board came past my desk; I wrote my name on the paper with a zero beside it and passed it on to the next person.

Happily, the morning sessions with Nanny continued. I think the difference was I was obsessed with the books I was reading, both at home and at school. My grandmother and mother and my aunt estimated that I was reading somewhere between 150 to 200 books a year. They were considered to be powerful, complex, scholarly, very intense and very meaningful. I guess they were referring to the great books I was reading like some of the books by Goethe, Emerson, Thoreau, Steinbeck, Somerset Maugham, Faulkner, Wolfe, and Hemingway, to name a few. For me, they were an escape and an outlet, but they were more than that; they had incredibly great things to say. Their ideas and books meant something and I felt an enormous kinship with them.

The teachers and I finally reached a truce. They wouldn't ask me to do any work and they finally quit sending me to the office. In turn, I caused no disturbances, read during class, and frequently ran errands for them.

For some reason, I was transferred to the school's band class. I think it was around October. The director was narcissistic and aggressive and didn't mind screaming at the array of children in his class. He finally made his way to me and he screamed at me. I took the drumsticks and stabbed them down through the drum and walked out of his room. For hundreds of students, it was recess time. The band director caught up with me, grabbed me by the shirt and told me that I wasn't going to walk away from him and that I was to go back inside. I think I hit him in the face twice and he went down on his back. The kids who witnessed all of this backed up and he walked way ahead of me to the principal's office. I followed him. I was told that I was expelled from school for two weeks, but a few minutes later the police department showed up and took me to the detention home.

They told me I was charged with assault and that it was a violation of my probation. Actually, that wasn't true. I had gotten off probation, so I suppose I was about to be put on probation for the second time. Anyway, I jumped a fence, caught several rides and went back to Nanny's house...or my house. That night, the officers came and brought me back to the detention home. The following morning, I met with a probation officer and was told I was being put back on probation for assaulting a teacher and escaping from the detention home; that was the first of what would eventually be 12 escapes.

Well, the year began and I suppose I became quite the entrepreneur as my stealing, shoplifting and burglary skills began to improve. As they did, all the kids at school wanted to buy things that I had stolen. From minor shoplifting, my stealing drastically increased to records, knives, more clothes, perfume, jewelry, watches. All these things were easy to sell to my classmates. In fact, I actually had to start carrying a notebook to keep up with the large number of orders as the word got around school. At Christmas, kids had asked for cameras, binoculars, and the males wanted weapons and clothes, but the girls wanted earrings, watches, bracelets. I found it interesting that there were as many girls that wanted to order things from me as there were males. The girls were also better at paying me. The money rolled in. I didn't need to rely on my grandparents. I bought my own cigarettes, paid for my own cab fare, bought my own food when needed. I even lent money with interest for a larger payback to other students.

However, I should inform the reader that I lived a very Spartan-like lifestyle. I had one pair of shoes, about three shirts, and only two pairs of blue jeans. But I was also able to pay for dozens of books that had historically been supplied by my grandmother, mother, and aunt.

The Christmas break was spent kind of like the summer. I ran the streets during the day with my group. We were in and out of restaurants, bars, and for me, stealing was the order of the day. I think it's important to mention that throughout all these different life activities I never failed to read every moment that I could, whether it was day, night, after Nanny and I talked in the morning, or from midnight to 3:00 in the morning by a small light to keep my grandfather from correcting me.

Halfway through the ninth grade and going on 14 years of age, I was living three separate lives…a lousy school life, life on the streets, and my life at home with Nanny and my grandfather. It's odd…it never dawned on me to misbehave at their house. I always acted like I was supposed to. I was extremely well-mannered and polite. I worked hard to please my grandmother and my grandfather. The whole family—my mother, my aunt, my two uncles, my grandparents and I—would traditionally have lunch at Nanny's house on Sundays. There were occasions when my uncles would correct me and also my mother might correct me about something I had done at school or in the community. I would typically make a sarcastic comment back to my uncles, thank my mother for her suggestion and do whatever I wanted to do. My grandparents had long since realized that my mother had no control over me and that I was not willing to be corrected by her. My grandparents were the only people from whom I accepted correction.

To the point of correction, let me explain. They never punished me. They never took away my freedom. They never spanked me. However, they never spared me from what they thought that I should know about how to live a correct life, but that's how it went. That was the way that I lived with them.

I think they felt that irrational force was useless if not just making things worse. I had never responded well to direct punishment after my father's beating and arrival at Nanny's house. Very few people had realized that but Nanny and my grandfather seemed to have a sixth sense about this.

During this period, I had periods of feeling very alone. There was a certain part of me that was losing contact with

> *"Remember George Fox, John Bunyan, and St. Augustine. And, don't forget, Lincoln lost more elections than any politician that ever ran. Milton was blind, Edison and Ford never finished school, and Napoleon Hill was a delinquent born in poverty. And Orison Marden didn't have a mother or a father, either."*
>
> **Nanny**

the general population. I spent a lot of time reading and thinking about what I had read. I was seriously drawn to books about great people who had done courageous things. I was beginning to find out certain things that seemed to put them all in the same group. They were great creators and great warriors and they also felt very different, often alone, and criticized for their beliefs. This was a revelation to me.

Stealing caught up with me in January. I had stolen some switchblade knives from Walgreen's on Third Street, downtown Baton Rouge. I went to jail, then to the detention home again, then to court in which I was informed that I was being put on probation for the third time. I remained in the detention home for a longer period than usual. The police were now honed in on me and I was now being transferred back and forth to answer questions about thefts, burglaries, and other crimes; or rather, not answering and avoiding their questions or giving them misleading answers...

There was one detective in particular, Officer Ray Thomas, who seemed very interested in me. His questioning was different than what other officers had done. He seemed to try to get to know what I was thinking and why I had done certain things, not just what I was being charged with. He took a personal interest in my situation. I was getting a bad reputation with the police department and particularly with the detective division.

Quite honestly, I think they had been convinced by Nanny I was redeemable. She had spoken personally with a number of them. I knew they had a deep respect for her. I think the original plans were to send me off to the Training Institute, but I think her communicating with them changed their plans.

I was picked up on numerous occasions for fighting. I was being treated like I had started the fights and would try to explain that that wasn't true. I had a fear of getting hurt, a fear of getting beat, and a fear of losing a fight, so if someone approached me who was threatening, it was like I would automatically start fighting to win. A number of assault charges were being added to my record as well as stealing, burglary, shoplifting. I was now being informed that I was a delinquent. By the end of the year, my time in jails and detention homes had increased. I had turned 14 in February.

There was a fair in town in Baton Rouge. My friends and I had chosen to attend. I stole the proceeds from the fair out of a box and we decided to use the funds to run away from home. Instead of hitchhiking, we jumped a train headed west. I remember that it was freezing on top of the train during the night and thinking that there had to be a better way to run away. Anyway, the train pulled in and stopped at Alexandria, Louisiana. We were spotted by somebody who managed the train yard and took off running. We were quickly surrounded by police cars who then took us to jail. Interestingly, the booking person's sponge had dried and he had to go try to find another one. While he went to go get one, we picked up brooms and told the police guard outside the cell, which led to a large front office lobby, the following…

I said to him, "Sweeping up and cleaning up, boss." He asked me who authorized that and I didn't answer. I just looked straight ahead like convicts do. I said, "Sweeping up the lobby, boss." He didn't say anything and so I threw the broom down and said, "To hell with it then."

He unlocked the cell door and said, "If they told you to sweep up the lobby, then sweep up the lobby." So we proceeded to sweep out the lobby all the way to the front door, down the front steps and then we ran. Naturally, an order went out to catch us. There was a school near-by and we stole some bicycles and then I stole a motor scooter. We tried to stick together but ended up being surrounded within about a two-block area. There were about 12 squad cars, lights flashing, surrounding our location and lots of cops attempting to run down through the neighborhood to catch us. Actually, they didn't catch any of us. We all got tired of running in the heat and just couldn't run anymore. We were transferred back to jail at which point each person's family was notified and came to pick us up in Alexandria. Instead of being released and brought downstairs, my grandmother came upstairs. The following is unbelievable: She told the sheriff to bring me some cleaner, water, and rags and told me to clean my jail cell first before I was released. She told them I didn't live in dirty circumstances at home and I wasn't going to live in dirty circumstances in jail. The task was completed and Nanny and my mother drove me home.

However, hold on!

I have never understood the following:

* Number one, I was never subpoenaed to come back to Alexandria for a jail escape. (This was my second escape.)

* Number two, or for resisting arrest.

* Number three, or for stealing bicycles and a motor scooter.

Later, these things show up in my record but with no consequence. All I can think of is Nanny's actions somehow must have thrown them off of what they would typically do because there was no court hearing after all of this.

But for the next week and a half Nanny asked me questions. "What was it like to ride on a train? What was it like to run away? Were you afraid? Or if you arrived in a strange city, how could you get a job? Where would you go? What would you do? How would you do it?" The questions made me realize the futility of running away. It's useless. You're running into a brick wall, but I had to learn the hard way.

School was over and it was now the beginning of June. The full summer loomed ahead. I had learned a lot of things in the past year and I wasn't sure what direction the summer was going to take. It turned out not to be so good...

Age: 14, summer after ninth grade
Location: Baton Rouge,
Louisiana

7

# Life in the streets began to be serious...

As I said, school was out. I hung with my friends. Had already run away and had already been put in jail. Apparently, that reputation travels through a pipeline to other city officers and police departments.

I found myself hanging out at the local bars, drinking beer, smoking cigarettes (about two packs a day), stealing and daily living in the streets.

I had learned some lessons from being in jail and detention homes and I was beginning to put them to great use. Stealing was second nature to me now and selling stolen items was easy if you knew the right people. My stealing went from shoplifting to breaking into cars, burglarizing

> *"There is loss, pain, failure, indifference, greed…*
> *But there is also greatness, honor, compassion and goodness.*
> *P.S. You only have two choices."*
>
> **Nanny**

businesses, and shoplifting more expensive items. If I was picked up for suspicion or questioning and put in jail, my jail mates were kind enough to pass on their pointers regarding stealing.

People on the streets and people I had gone to school with became regular customers.

My probation officer pushed me to get a job. The first job that I got was at a grocery store. The guy who owned it was especially cruel and picked on the mentally-handicapped Afro-American delivery boy. He made him cry almost every day. I threw his cash register on the floor, told him I quit and told him how I felt about him. He ran to the front door and, as I went out the door, he pushed me. I then grabbed him by the shirt, pulled him outside the store and hit him about six times. He also got in one good lick on me. My cheek started to swell. But after he got knocked down, he ran inside and called the police. They picked me up and kept me overnight. I was charged with aggravated battery. However, I guess he dropped charges because I didn't hear any more about it.

Next job was at the famous root beer stand uptown. Everyone in Baton Rouge knew where this root beer stand was; it was at the corner of Government St. and St. Ferdinand. Well, anyway, on the second day I'm late as usual and he fires me in the morning. So there were three other people working there that day and I put up a sign saying everything was free. While the other kids my age shook their heads and laughed, the parking lot was full of excited mothers and children. We gave away every ice cream cone, every bag of potato chips, every mug of root beer in the entire store. At that point, one of the people who worked there gave me a ride home. Surprise, surprise…a squad car came to Nanny's house the following morning. I think the owner claimed losses into the thousands of dollars or something like that. My comment to the detectives who interviewed me was, "So sorry. Just happened to be broke."

I spent one night in a detention home, was brought back for another interrogation, and told I was free to go. Also, strangely, I remember that even though I had given his belongings away from the store window, there was some odd legal technicality about firing me that morning or giving the stuff away or not paying me for the time that I spent there. Actually, I don't remember. I just remember that I never went to court for those charges either. And technically, if I had been charged, the family members that worked there with me that day would have had to have been charged as well. I did get a very penetrating interview from my probation officer along with the detectives. Then after that, I went down to Ligget's Drugstore and got a chocolate malt.

My third employment experience was at a motel. I supplemented my income by selling liquor out of the back of my car to people at the motel. It was very easy to do. The back of my car was filled with liquor, snacks, sex books, cigarettes, every form of cold drinks and sweets.

This process was especially good when there were tourist attractions in Baton Rouge and the motel was full of not only people but drunk people who were easy to sell to. A few weeks later I was fired, of course. The owner accused me of stealing out of his register, but actually, I didn't do that. What I did was unplug all of his vending machines so I was the sole 'grocery and liquor store' from evening until 2:00 and 3:00 in the morning.

In between that, of course, I went to parties, social gatherings, dances, bars. While I did get involved in frequent fights, I was pulled in and interrogated for all fights and any type of incident that happened in the area.

However, they also knew I would never tell or 'rat' on anybody for anything. I guess they got a kick out of attempting to break me.

It's a good time to mention that there are some things that I didn't do. I never pulled an armed robbery with a weapon. I never raped anyone. I never hurt a child. I never broke into a family home. I never hit anyone smaller than me.

My arrest record grew. The things that started getting added to it were under-age drinking, suspicion of forgery, interrogation for stolen property, hitting a much older man in the face with a beer bottle at the bar who was trying to hit me, and escaping from the police after they had placed me in one of their cars.

I never paid for anything and my knowledge of how to do that increased with every visit to jail and detention. I learned to buy a tooth and carry a little insect in a plastic container in my pocket so that when I ate at a restaurant I would stand up and announce that I had found an insect or a broken tooth in my food. I would say it loud enough to usually get permission to get a free meal at a later date. I mean it's just a way of not having to go home during the day so you can eat while you're living in the streets.

Back to my arrest record. In Baton Rouge, the hot weather grew hotter. I ran with my friends. My arrests and jail times increased. There was never a shortage of customers who were willing to pay for the stolen goods I could get my hands on. Transportation wasn't that great of a problem; nevertheless, I did steal some motor scooters.

Another round of intensive interrogations and questioning by detectives took place from middle to late July. I knew that my group was 'solid,' which meant they didn't 'rat' on others. However, the interrogation questions were getting pretty specific about things that I had stolen on certain dates at certain locations, how much and how many and even where. I wondered where they were getting their information. Maybe from the kids that I had sold stuff to who had not been the people who ran with me on the streets? Or someone on the rim of our group who was telling everything they knew about me? They reminded me that the aggravated battery, passing out goods from the root beer stand, fights, and other burglaries and shoplifted items were a violation of my probation and would all be entered into my record. At this point, I wasn't keeping up with the number of interviews I was required to come to where I was interrogated and then released. Things seemed to be getting more serious.

In August, more than one interview took place. In early August on one occasion I was questioned for about six hours straight by about six to seven people. They were even more specific about things that I had stolen from construction sites, siphoning gas, shoplifting. *How did they get this information?*

The first week of August, must have been my second interview, they said they had details of my shoplifting at five different stores, could charge me with six to ten cases of assault, several cases of aggravated battery, burglary, breaking and entering, selling stolen items, resisting arrest, excessive probation violations.

To this day, I don't know how they were able to find out all of those details. It certainly looked like a team had gone out and questioned dozens of people regarding their interactions with me.

Of course, I never confessed to any single one of these items.

I hated the questioning. I hated the police. It was one thing to be questioned about the things I had done, but I hated the accusations of things that I had never been involved with and I know they knew it.

On one day, they sent in a new guy. It was obvious to me that he was new. Maybe he had just been hired as a detective. So the guy informed me that he was going to be very, very rough and wouldn't put up with any foolishness from me, so the quicker I came clean the better off I would be. I was quiet for a few minutes and then I told him that I understood, that he scared me and that I would confess. I went into detail about stealing eight cars. (Of course, all of it was a lie.)

A slight smirk came across his face as he wrote down detail after detail of everything I had to say about the eight stolen cars I had just admitted to taking. It turns out that he spent that next week, the week that was originally set aside for his honeymoon, investigating each of the incidents to which I had confessed. All of his time and effort and missed honeymoon led him to the realization that I had sent him on a wild goose chase, that none of the thefts had ever happened. I had gotten him good. The next time I saw the young detective he was seething. It took two people to hold him down while he was calling me names.

It was my turn to smirk. "You need to remember I'm a juvenile. You're not supposed to hit me."

That angered him all the more with accusations that I had ruined his honeymoon.

I stared straight at him. "No, you ruined it. However, you did learn what it's like to interview, you know, a young sociopath from the streets when you think you're so damned good and tough. Basically, you're just narcissistic and new to your field but you feel people are just going to sit there and tell you everything that they ever did. So, since you felt like that then, okay, it wasn't my fault. Basically, it was yours. Tell your wife that you're so sorry that you're narcissistic, stupid and naïve." The officers, while laughing, had to hustle him out of the room before his fury could break him free from their hold to hit me.

The scheduling of interviews in early August grew in number, in seriousness, and in intensity. About six different people were rotated as my investigators, one of them revealing to me that I had about 14 yellow legal-size tablet pages listing all that I had been arrested for and what I had done, including witnesses. The questions were getting more pointed and the answers were getting more recorded. These people were serious and I was picking up on that fact. I was informed by the probationary division about mid-August that a court hearing was going to be set for late August or early September, but there would be a couple of more interviews before that date.

They informed me that all of my arrests and charges and probation violations, problems in school and aggression towards people at school as well as in the community would be brought before the judge at that time. *Okay. Obviously, they had been doing a study on me for quite some time.* It was emphasized that my appearance in court was mandatory, that I could bring any family members or legal counsel.

A day or two later, they picked me up and put me in jail before the impending court case. Jail and then the detention home. They stated that I had escaped from the detention home before, had broken out of jail in Alexandria, had stolen vehicles and that I was a flight risk. The detention home people let me call Ray Thomas in the juvenile division. He had me released and brought back to Nanny's house to stay until the trial date.

*I was going to have trouble talking to Nanny about this.*

Age:14
Location: Baton Rouge,
Louisiana

8

# "I'm hurt, but I'm not surprised"...

The court date had been set. I sat quietly on the back porch for about a day and a half. Nanny handed me a cup of coffee and said, "Let's talk about it." She knew something was wrong.

I told her all the charges that they had discussed with me and that I had a terrible feeling about the up and coming court hearing. I told her, "I guess I have run as far up against the system that is allowable."

She said, "I'm hurt, but I'm not surprised."

I pretty much told her what had gone on in the interrogations and court interviews, what I had stolen and things I had done. She listened, made breakfast, and we had more coffee.

I told her that I had hidden things under the pillars of the house such as cameras, knives, and other stolen items. She said she knew and she had put them in bags and wondered what I was going to do with them. I looked at her and just said, "I want to make sure they are never discovered here."

If I were to describe her reaction, it seemed to be concern and sadness, but noticeably, she was more sad for me and the consequences I was facing. I stayed home until the court date, found the bags full of stolen items and went out on the back porch to talk to her. I asked Nanny to please not accompany me and she said, "I understand."

I didn't want to see my beloved grandmother in front of a judge. She had been so patient, so caring, and had taught me so much about freedom, greatness, goodness. I needed her to let me go alone. If there was a price to pay, there would be nothing she could do to stop it. Like I said, she looked at me long and hard, put her hand on my cheek and said, "I understand."

The day of the court hearing, I got a ride to the police station and went to the juvenile division. I sat two sets of bags down and told the detective, "These are for Mr. Ray Thomas."

He said, "Did you steal these?"

I said, "I didn't say I stole them. I said they are for Mr. Ray Thomas." I was then escorted through the department out the back to the courtroom. Entering the court, the officer showed me where to sit and wait while another case was being heard. After that case, the judge's attention was directed at me. He said, "Are you, Darryl Wheat?"

I said, "Yes, sir."

He said, "Come through the doors there and sit at the table." Several minutes passed as he was writing something at his desk and he directed me to stand before the court. "So you're Darryl Wheat, aren't you? You're my next case."

I said, "I guess so. I don't know what your schedule is."

"Your file is very big. In fact, it's one of the biggest juvenile files I've ever seen." He said, "Did you hear me?"

I said, "Yes, sir."

"Did you do all these things, all these misdemeanors, and felonies listed on this record in front of me?"

"Your Honor, I never said I did any of them. I guess they're the writings of the police and the detective division."

"I repeat," said the judge. "Do you admit you did all of this?"

"No, Your Honor. I'm not admitting to anything or any one of them." "I'm asking you again. Did you do these things that you're being accused of doing?"

I said, "Your Honor, you seem to know more about this than I do. I don't suppose my feelings or beliefs have anything to do with this case, actually."

He looked up at me with seriousness. He didn't seem angry. He left the file the way it was and leaned back in the chair. He said, "I heard that you were a great baseball player. As a matter of fact, most of the people around here have gone to see you play. You've been written up in the newspaper, on television." He stopped and he looked at me. I guess he was waiting for me to say something.

"Okay."

He said, "How did you go from that to what I'm reading?"

I said, "Your Honor, I don't think that what I have to say is going to have much bearing on what this court is going to do."You could hear a penny drop in the courtroom. Apparently, I wasn't supposed to say or talk to the judge the way I was talking to him. It was like I'd done something wrong The silence was broken by the judge."Why didn't you bring your mother or father with you?"

I said, "Why? What purpose would that serve?"

He looked at me, looked down, took a deep breath, and then leaned forward in his chair.

I said to myself, *Here it comes.*

His voice was impassionate and terse. "I'm sentencing you to the Louisiana Training Institute for Boys."

I said, "I'm not surprised. I would assume you came here with that thought already in mind."

At that point, my mother opened the door of the courtroom, entered and walked up to the judge, advocating for me not to be sent to the Institute. I had no idea she was coming. Only Nanny could have told her. The judge knew Nanny and P.V., my uncle and Mama's brother.

The judge knew him well, saying things like, "Well, I'll be darned. You're Mildred, P.V.'s sister. So this is Mrs. Slocum's grandson. Well, I didn't know that and," he told my mother, "I've already sentenced him and I can't take the sentence back."

I smiled a little bit after that because I thought he had not sent in the paperwork and the hearing wasn't even over, so it's a little hard to believe what he told my mother. Mother started crying. I finally got her to leave. She was trying to comfort me saying that she would visit L.T.I. that was the last thing I wanted her to do. I remember telling her, "Please don't. Just let me get through this. I'll find a way to call you."

My mother kissed me on the cheek and hugged me and said, "I'm sorry."

I shook my head and said, "Hey, my fault. Comfort Nanny. She'll be devastated."

My time in front of the judge was over. The decision had been made regarding my next move. An officer led me to a long bench in the hallway outside of the courtroom and made it very clear that my reputation for running away was well known and I was not to move from that spot. For 30 minutes I stayed put, and then I had to use the bathroom which was right across the hall from me. About 9:30 AM, I went into the bathroom and, about 10:30 a.m., all kinds of commotion started happening while I was in there. I cracked open the window and looked down from the second floor to see people shouting instructions and running. Sirens were going off. I had no idea what was happening but I had been told to stay put. I took time for a cigarette before settling back into my assigned spot in the hall. No one was around. Totally vacated. So I waited. Alone. From 10:30 AM to about 11:30 when a police officer walked down the hall. I got his attention and asked if I was going to have anything to eat or drink brought to me, or how was all of this supposed to work.

"Who are you?" "Darryl Wheat."

There was a quick gasp. "Oh, Lord. Good Lord. The entire city is being blocked off and looking for you!" He yelled for backup.

There was no answer when I asked, since it was noontime, for a hot dog, hamburger or chili. Not only was there no answer, the officers acted like I was Al Capone, seemed very nervous and serious, and loaded me in the back of a squad car along with two other boys who, apparently, had also been sentenced to the detention home. Immediately upon arrival, I was taken to the solitary cage at the detention home.

All of this because I went to the bathroom? The answer I got was that they felt like I was an escape risk.

At approximately 2:30, I began faking chest pains and a stomachache. The house parents checked on me and I took advantage, shutting them into the cage and locking them in. "Darryl, please don't do this. You are going to get into more trouble."

I laughed. "How is that possible?"

I used the master key to let everyone out of their rooms in the home, including one that was termed "crazy." He really wasn't crazy but had gotten that label by doing some silly things in the classroom and showing off. When the police showed up, I went outside and told them that the crazy person was holding the mother and father of the detention home hostage, could even kill them. The officers already there backed off and called for assistance. Shortly, we could count four, then six, then ten squad cars with their lights all flashing at the front gate. The number kept increasing.

Meanwhile, inside the home, the detainees had made personal choices with what to do with their now free time. Some were watching television. Some phone calls were placed to families. One black female decided she wanted pancakes and made enough to pile the home's kitchen table about two feet high with pancakes. No plates, just pancakes. About half a bucket of syrup and melted butter were added to make a huge mess that dripped onto the floor! We could go in there and get one and eat it when we wanted to. They were fantastic!

The police still surrounded the home and I was called out periodically to talk with them. I was told to disarm the crazy person or they would come in and do it for me. I said, "If you do that, he could kill them. Let me handle this." This continued for about four hours. They bought it. It was a standoff while the parents were actually safely in the cage meant me, and the kids were doing whatever they wanted. No one was being hurt or threatened but the police had quite a different impression, anxious and concerned about the welfare of the detention home parents.

Frank Thomas from the juvenile division appeared at the gate and asked to speak to me by himself. He asked me to come over about ten to 15 feet from the other police officers. Frank said, "They have a guy over there by the water tower with a rifle who's going to shoot you if you don't end this. Are the people okay?"

I said, "Sure. I just locked them in there and fed them supper and everything."

Frank said, "Darryl, I want you to stop this before somebody gets hurt."

I said, "Okay, Mr. Thomas. Give me five to ten minutes to go back in there and fix everything." I went back inside and undid everything that had been done. Everyone went back to their rooms, whether they liked it or not. I locked them back in. Then I went outside and opened the gate for the police.

Police poured in from everywhere. I was put back into solitary and then cuffed and chained, hands and waist. Two locks were put on my door. I asked the detention home mother if I could still have supper. She must have found that funny because she shook her head and laughed.

Two men arrived early the next morning and asked me if I was Darryl Wheat. I replied that I was. It turned out that they were on special assignment to transport me and the other two boys who had been sentenced yesterday. They said their usual transports were to Angola, not to L.T.I., but they had been hired because of me and warned about my behavior and past history of escape and that they were prepared.

I said, "Whatever. Are you sure two people are enough?"

*I will never forget that last night at the detention home. The night before I was to be transferred to the Institution to start serving my time. Daddy brought me this Bible. He told me all I had to do was pray. My God in heaven! This was supposed to make up for all I had learned and suffered in the streets, all my fears, nights alone, nightmares, fishing trips never taken, rodeos never seen, and instruction, guidance, and support never given? And what of love, love so lost, so forever buried? But to top it off, the incredible and unbelievable icing on the cake, he told me that if he had gone to court with me that I would not be going to reform school. His impractical reasoning is second only to his deteriorated compassion. His judgment, when it comes to his child, irrevocably impaired, and his lack of acceptance of me as his son, his flesh and blood, irreconcilable.*

***Darryl***

The chains were wrapped twice around my waist and attached to the handcuffs but were long enough for me to smoke a cigarette. The three of us were loaded into the back seat of the transport. The one next to me decided to give me a lecture about my attitude and how, if I cooperated with authority, I could probably get out sooner.

I looked over at him. "Are you absolutely and unequivocally stupid?"

> *Instead of handing you his love and parenting...he gave you a Bible. I believe you came out ahead. I think you got the best of the deal.*
>
> ***Nanny***

We are going to a juvenile correctional institute that is maximum security in the middle of nowhere." Apparently, he hadn't been to one before.

He still continued. "You need to change and cooperate with L.T.I." That was far enough. I hit him with all my might with my elbow right in the face and blood went everywhere. I don't think I broke his nose but the officer driving pulled over and a shotgun was pulled out. I stayed on the right side of the seat; the other guy was put on the far side with the third guy being in the middle.

*A shotgun to bring juveniles to a training institute? Heavens!*

The officer who had broken up the fight grabbed me by the throat and threatened that if there was a next time he would take me from the car and make sure that I never did it again.

I said, "So you're used to bringing adults to the state prison and now you're bringing three juveniles to L.T.I. Does it make any difference to you? And what about the chains around me and my being one-third your size? Does that mean anything to you?"

His response was, "No, it doesn't and you'll find that out."

"Whatever."

En route, we stopped for something to eat without incident. Heading back to the car, something on the ground caught my eye. It was a key. When I started leaning down to pick it up. one of the boys said, "Wheat! Wheat, don't!" I looked at him without bending further. He directed my attention to one of the guards who had the shotgun leveled at me.

The guard had been ready. "Oh, thought you were going to get the key and escape?" I figured out that the kid had basically saved my life. The rest of our trip to L.T.I. continued without any problems.

Age: 14
Location: Louisiana Training
Institute

# 9

# The fences were topped with barbed wire, not a pretty sight when you're 14 years of age...

Around mid-afternoon, we arrived at the Louisiana Training Institute. The two officers loaded themselves back into the car and one couldn't keep from making a nasty comment. "See you in Angola!"

I said, "Probably because you're a pedophile and like juveniles."

He frowned and said, "I'll be damned glad to see you there." Their car exited through the front gate.

First up on the agenda of my new life...I am to go and meet with the superintendent of L.T.I. I'm sure this is routine. He looks at me and says, "I'm looking forward to seeing you play on thc baseball team.

I said, "I'm not going to play on your baseball team."

He said, "Really? We'll have to talk more about that, you and me."

I said, "There's nothing to talk about. I'm not playing on your baseball team."

His face got a little tenser and his voice a little more precise. "You will learn that there are a lot of things around here that you'll have to do that you don't like to do, Darryl Wheat."

Next up was a visit to the social worker, a very nice female. She wanted to make conversation and achieve some friendly bond. I wasn't having any part of it. I said, "I'm not under any illusion. This is not a group home or a place where therapy, assistance, or any form of protection exists. I understand that this is a juvenile penitentiary and I'm not filled with irrational illusions. I've been in jail before."

She said, "I know you have. I know that you've had some family problems and I'd like to talk to you about some of the issues you've had."

I said, "Really? You're going to help me? No offense, you seem like a nice lady, but I don't think this place and I are going to get along very well."

She said, "Darryl, I really care what happens to you."

I said, "Don't waste your time. Let's be serious, this is a juvenile prison."

I was ushered out of her office, out and onto 'the square.' Buildings surrounded the square, cottages, et cetera. Kids were coming in off crews, 10 and 12 to a truck. And, as they passed by, there were catcalls and whistles. "New meat! New meat! Hey, look, we've got new meat!" It was the typical prison welcome mat.

I looked up at them and smiled as each truck went by. I was used to those reactions.

It was my understanding that I had been assigned to E-Cottage. Apparently, that's where they confined the 'bad boys' from what I was told at the time of my assignment. From the square, I walked directly across from the administration building to meet my house parent, Mr. Moody. I was shown my locker but no lock was supplied and I didn't have one on me. I was told to be careful if I didn't have a lock, things would be taken out. I said, "Okay." He was surprised, I think, that I didn't make in-depth conversation.

Shortly, the people from E-Cottage began to show up and he announced to me that everyone would be getting ready for supper and to prepare to do the same. There were 50 boys to a cottage. The other 49 were coming in. I was number 50.

I went into the locker room, I guess just by instinct, and stood next to my locker. To my left, one guy commented, "Hey, that's a beautiful blue shirt. Don't you think that's a beautiful blue shirt he has on?"

As I looked to the left of me, I was aware that some of the kids were positioning themselves, one looking out for the guards, one coming at me and one in between coming at me. My street shirt, which was nice looking and blue, of course, was the target. They wanted it. I was new meat. I was supposed to be scared. From jail and detention homes, I knew the game. They wanted my shirt and were going to teach me what my position was in the cottage.

I waited for the first boy to get right next to me before I hit him with all my might. Fortunately, he went down. The second kid that was in the middle was able to come straight ahead and swing on me and his punch grazed the top of my head, but I connected on him several times sending him across the room against the wall. The first boy was beginning to get up. I kicked him in the head and he went back down on the floor. The third boy ran out of the locker room door and into the cottage that I was to live in. There were about 50 chairs in the room, one for each kid. I went to the door and saw that he had run to the left and took off after him. I dove across the table and got some good 'licks' in on him.

Mr. Moody entered the room, looked around and wanted to know immediately what the problem was. I didn't say anything. One of the boys that was a 'rat' said, "Those three started it. I think they wanted his shirt."

No punishment was issued and no instructions were given at all. He said, "Everyone get in line and start counting off. It's time to go to supper."

I counted off and we all walked in a straight line towards the cafeteria. Everybody in the line was sizing me up and stealing glances at me. I did overhear this; I didn't know whether it was good or bad. "That's the guy over there. He just got through hitting three boys in the cottage."

Typical to my life, in about three hours I had ceased to be anonymous.

With supper over, each cottage's residents lined up and headed back to their own dormitories. After arriving, we all stripped down to our underwear and picked a chair to sit in. We listened to the radio, played cards, read out-of-date magazines. Bathroom visits were one at a time; two were never to go at any given time. Fearful 'rats' hung around Mr. Moody, the house parent, those afraid of the cottage's population. The house parent would leave and the next person that would come would be the person that was the guard for the night dormitory, which was upstairs. He was called a night watchman. The room contained 50 beds and, while there were rules, one person in the bathroom at a time and not getting out of your bed without permission, as you would expect, the night watchman just went to sleep in the doorway.

We counted off before going upstairs. We counted off after we got upstairs. Lights went out. The watchman was at his post and the sad and pathological night starts. Dreams caused some children to talk, others to cry. Some were whimpering. Some were asking for their mamas. Hard to ignore and hard to sleep the first night. There's aggression. One kid gets up, hits another kid three times hard, goes back to bed. My defenses are up the rest of the night not knowing if I'm someone's target or not.

## Day two dawns…

We counted off before we were allowed to go to either the locker room or a room designed for state-supplied pants, shirts, shoes. A message was delivered for me to come to the administration building. I also received a second message that I was supposed to be attending school that morning.

Missed breakfast. An escort took me to the school. I had a good look at the chain-link fences topped with barbed wire. Well done.

My first class was math. You won't believe it; the textbooks were fourth, fifth and sixth-grade math books. I was 14 years old, supposed to be in the tenth grade, but the math book handed to me was on a third or fourth-grade level; addition, subtraction. It was just stupid. I made a negative comment to the instructor. He, in turn, asked me to state my name. He said, "Stand up and say something about yourself."

I said, "I'm alive. I'm here. I'm under your jurisdiction complete with barbed wire. What else do you want?" and sat down.

He took a couple of steps toward me and said, "I want you to say a part of your history to this class."

I said, "No, I'm not going to do that." I was sent to the principal's office. He said I would have to be more cooperative and that he would let the incident pass without using a paddle on me this time.

After lunch, there was gym class, or what normal schools would call P.E., physical education. Not here. This was a time for the guards to amuse themselves. From the school, people took their seats in the bleachers. The only activity that went on in P.E. was boxing. Everybody cheered on the sidelines for who they wanted to win. I shouldn't have been surprised when I was quickly selected to be one of the contenders. We used boxing gloves. My opponent was about 25 or 30 pounds heavier than I was and about six inches taller. Strangely, his nickname was PeeWee. There was no ring, it was just the basketball gym floor.

Adrenaline hit me like a thunderbolt. The signal came. We started. PeeWee swung. I ducked and hit him four times, knocking him down. The coach broke us up, wiped off both sets of gloves, and signaled for us to continue to box. PeeWee and I traded about five punches to the face, then I knocked him down again for the second time. Before the coach could get there, he started backing up and running around the gym and I started running after him. I had lost it. I was full of adrenaline, terrified, afraid of losing, and had no idea about when to quit. The coach grabbed me. I jerked loose from him. I said, "Let me finish the job. You wanted us to fight."

I think the coach could tell something was wrong with me. He covered me and held me and said, "Listen to me when I talk. Are you okay?"

I couldn't speak. I was taking deep breaths. I was starting to come back to the present.

PeeWee was coming towards me with a smile. He said, "I can't believe you just did that. You fight good, man. You're cool." Raised his hands in a high five. He said, "Man, can you fight!" We became friends for the rest of my time there.

Mumbling was going on all around the gym referring to what everyone had just witnessed. What I did and how crazy I got and not wanting to stop and screaming to let me go to finish the fight was being whispered all around. I had no idea whether this was a good idea being spread around or a bad idea being spread around. But now the cottage and people in my school were beginning to talk about me. Good or bad? Which direction was this taking?

## Night number two...

Several boys tried to make conversation with me. I wouldn't. You don't do that until you know who they are. No defenses down. No playing the game. They could be 'rats' or trying to learn where your weak spots are.

Count off standing by the bed. Get in the bed. Lights out. Same sounds as last night except one addition. A guy nicknamed Red went to the bathroom while a little boy was in the bathroom. From my bunk, I can see that he makes him perform oral sex. The smaller boy cries.

Red gave him two cigarettes like it was a reward. Didn't sit well with me at all. Didn't seem fair. I didn't like it at all. I pitied the smaller boy.

## Morning number two…

My second L.T.I. morning. Downstairs. Get dressed. Go to the door. Line up in order. Or get hit, slapped, or kicked. Count off. On to the cafeteria for breakfast.

Several cottages ate together, but E-Cottage was supposed to eat with each other as a group. I noticed all the tables seemed to be full except one table with one chair empty. From behind me, the guard said, "Find a chair and sit down now."

I went over to the one chair and sat down. As I took my seat, I noticed a sense of anxiety around the table. Across from me was a large boy, probably around 5'11", about 250 pounds, and noticeably one of the largest boys in the room, let alone our cottage. One boy to the left spoke up, "Hey, Fatty. Aren't you going to take new meat's biscuit?"

I'm new. Obviously my biscuit.

He says in a deep voice, "Uh, yeah. I'm going to have to have your biscuit."

These scenes and actions when you're incarcerated, as many times as I have been, are nothing new. I looked up at him and said, "Let me get this straight. Since I'm the new meat here, I guess you get to take my biscuit."

**November 1956**

**Dear Nanny,**

*Thought I'd just drop a line from my classroom. This school is teaching me things. Things I never found in a public library. I am learning about the many colored, uneven fragments of the glass mind of the homosexual, the disguised need of the compulsive thief, the precedent events that come before the blatant, fearless, ruthless armed robbery, the crumbled and spilled emotions of the eventual suicide who someday in the future will jump into the swirling current of a river or walk calm and deliberately in front of the hot, pounding steel of the locomotive, who will slide off the ledge of the skyscraper, who will put the revolver barrel snug to the skull just above the ear.*

***Darryl***

He's shaking his head up and down, yes. "You're right."

I said, "I see. I just wanted to make sure I had it right." Of importance was the fact that the tables furnished by the State had that old silver rim around the edge and kind of a rubber inlay in the table, rubber kind of like a hard clay. I looked him in the eye and he looked me in the eye and I placed my biscuit in the center of the table between our trays. When he reached for the biscuit and his hand was on it, I took my fork and ran it through his hand with all of my might. He tried pulling his hand away and couldn't; the fork was deeply embedded in the table. And the unbelievable shock was registering, not only on his face but on every face sitting at the table who had just witnessed this aggressive act.

With my knife (barely as sharp as a butter knife), I put it to his throat and said, "You 'rat' on me and this won't be the end of this."

He hollered for a guard because of the pain. Blood was coming from the top and under his hand. They proceeded to get him up from the table and, of course, take him to the hospital.

I looked at the other boys at the table and said, "Does anybody have a problem here?" They just shook their heads. There weren't any verbal responses. I had already confiscated the fork from the boy to my right and had it in my hand. An act like this doesn't go unnoticed by the inmates in the room; maybe the guards but never the inmates. The incident and my name were circulating in the room. I was making a name for myself. Of course, that's dangerous because it's only going to be respected as *leave me alone* or carry with it unexpected retribution. I had no idea how I was being perceived but I wasn't willing to put up with any of their behaviors, threats, or intimidation.

Was I scared? Yes.

Was I terrified? Yeah.

Hyper-alert and vigilant? You're not kidding.

Had I done the right thing? Absolutely.

You either take up for yourself or you're a punk. You don't just lose your biscuit, cigarettes, freedom, family gifts from home.

> *You do what you have to do to survive.*
>
> **Nanny**

And the fights start off with the assumption they can beat you.

Fatty didn't 'rat' on me. He came back with stitches in his hand, sat with his group. At one point, I walked over to him and said, "Everything okay?"

And he said, "Yeah."

That's a reform school signal that the issue is over.

## Day number two and back to school...

I stated the books were stupid. Sent to the office again. I asked Mr. Youngblood, the principal, if there was a library within the facility, a place that I could get some books. He said, "No. But that's not what you're here for. You're here for sassing the teacher and you're violating rules, not just here from what I hear. I'm going to have to paddle you," he informed me.

I said, "No. If you hit me with that board, I will fight you back. I've already been hit by my father and you're not going to hit me with that board."

Taking it all in, Mr. Youngblood leaned back in his chair. He finally said, "You're making this hard on yourself. You're extremely bright. I'm up to date on your file. You do understand that if you leave the school you will be put on a crew and you will not be allowed to ever return to school. If you mess up on a daily crew, then you'll be placed on Mr. Walker's detention crew. They work in the swamps, highway, in the corn that cuts you to pieces, in the rain, sleet, snow. You're one step away from that, so why don't you just take your licks and let it go?"

I said, "No."

"You will defend yourself and start a fight?" he asked. "Yes, you can bet on it."

"You won't take your licks?"

"No." I looked at him straight in the face. I was dead serious.

He said, "Well, your alternative then is to work inside the institution or somewhere. Come with me."

We didn't go to a field; he took me to the administration building. From there, they transferred me to a machine shop where I stayed until noon. Being placed in the machine shop had been one strange turn of events. The coach came and got me and took me to the gym.

"I understand that you play basketball and you're pretty good at it."

I said, "So?"

He said, "Okay, shoot a few baskets." After I shot a few times, he said, "Okay. I'm going to make you first team and you're going to play forward."

Potential problems continued to arise each day. I fended them off one by one. At times the problems were verbal, at times they were physical. The next few days I practiced with the basketball team during lunch hours and evenings. I spent the mornings at the machine shop. I had not yet experienced a crew but had heard that I would probably be assigned to Mr. Austin's crew at a later date.

There was a basketball game that Friday afternoon and the first string people were supposed to practice before the game started. It was common for the guys in the machine shop to make rings out of scrap metal that might be lying around. Everyone knew that demerits would be received if any metal left the machine shop, let alone anything such as rings that could be made to be used for protection. They were highly valued. Even pieces of steel could be made into knives and hidden under your shoe, in your hair, in a book you were holding, and so forth.

One boy gave me his that was almost finished and I was in the process of making one for myself when I was searched and it was found.

I was told that I couldn't play basketball or practice that afternoon because of the ring.

I tried to tell the manager of the machine shop that I was on the first string and he said, "Well, tough. You're not going."

To make it worse, he took the rest of the boys over to watch the practice and locked me in the machine shop.

He had brought his new 1956 Mercury into the machine shop to be washed, polished and worked on by the kids in the shop. The car and I were there alone and locked up together. While he and the boys attended the practice, I took my anger out on his car. I bashed in his front and back windshields, the door windows, headlights, backlights, tore off his steering wheel, and I don't remember what else. I do remember the door to the machine shop being opening up after the practice was over and the kids who had attended were with him. Everyone stopped in complete silence. I walked up to him and said, "I told you not to leave me in here."

He walked past me to his car and got down on his hands and knees and I could swear he was crying. All I could hear from him was, "My new car, my new car."

I was sent to the cottage to be watched over by the house parent the rest of the afternoon. Again, a reaction went across the Institute like it was on a neon marquee. As the kids pulled in from supper many of them asked me did I really do it or how did I do it or what did I do. I said, "I bashed in his damn automobile."

Count off. Supper. Eat. Return. Boring. Except for the fact that apparently, I was the topic of conversation.

The next morning, I was escorted to the administration building. I went before what's called The Demerit Committee composed of administrative people which included a social worker and one main guy who ran the committee who worked in the administration building. They re-informed me about the relationship between merits and demerits. If you receive 100 merits, the judge is usually in approval of release. I was given 25 demerits for the destruction of the car and 25 demerits for making the ring. After this, my count was at a negative 50. (And I had just gotten there!) I was reminded that that meant almost two months longer on my sentence. I thanked the head of the Demerit Committee for his generosity and told him I would take him out for lunch some time. He looked shocked and said, "You sass me and I'll give you demerits for that."

I said, "Excuse me. I was just trying to be companionable or whatever."

As I wasn't allowed back in the machine shop, a new job was found for me. I was to clean the home of the automobile's owner, who lived on campus, as a punishment. His wife didn't push me to do any of the housework. We actually had intelligent conversations. They had a collection of books, so I got to read some books. This only lasted a few weeks because he quit his job and then moved.

The time came for me to report to Austin's crew and I considered him the only guy in the entire institution that was kind, considerate, decent, reasonable, and a great human being who actually cared for the children. There were lots of tasks that we took on: picking up leaves, de-feathering and cutting up chickens for meals, break-ing up concrete on the property. That didn't keep the number of fistfights down though. Those still occurred regularly with either someone from another cottage or a random kid on campus. My merit count stayed a nega-tive number with all the incidents that involved me. But I was not at issue with Mr. Austin. He watched me but trusted me. I never tried to run away on his crew. I liked him and respected him.

Unfortunately, one of the fights caused me to be trans-ferred away from Mr. Austin's crew and onto Walker's crew. This was an entirely different experience. I was not a fan of Mr. Walker and he was not a fan of mine. I was punished immediately after being transferred to his crew. He took me over to a very small building with tools in it. He told me to take the tools out. I did. And he took a bucket of muddy water and threw it against the wall, ceiling, and floor and told me to clean it up. It was hard work but I got it done and I was proud of the results of my effort. Mr. Walker showed up, looked at it, threw another bucket of mud and water against the same wall, ceiling and floors. He told one of the guards, "It looks dirty to me. Clean it again," and walked away.

Okay. Then that's the Mr. Walker I had heard about. As soon as he turned his back, I left out the door and walked calmly through the bushes like everything was okay and, as soon as Walker was out of sight, I went over the fence. I ran across the street to the top of the levee next to the river. There was an Afro-American man with a team of horses. I told him to get down and let me have the wagon because I was running away. He got down and I used the strap to try to get the horses going. I said, "Giddy up. Go, team. Let's go, horses." I thought it might get me away from the area soon. He tapped me on the shoulder.

I said, "Would you please? Can't you see I'm trying to run away?" Being a city boy didn't help me one bit. 'Giddy up' and 'go team' didn't help the horses go forward at all.

He tapped me on the shoulder again.

I said, "Please. I'm trying to get away here. You can have your horses back in a few minutes." By that time, there were cars and people coming from both the front and the back towards me. I wasn't going to be going anywhere.

He tapped me on the shoulder and said, "All you had to do was push this lever forward and the horses would go forward."

I had to laugh. I said to him, "That's probably why all of us are in here: impulsive, don't listen and have bad judgment."

He patted me on the back and gave me a cigarette. That was my first runaway.

The following morning, The Demerit Committee. I guess I had a genius for making correctional people angry because as The Demerit Committee came to my case, the head of the committee asked me why I ran away. And I told him I had not been enjoying my stay here, at which point everyone but him started laughing. He was incensed, assuming everyone wasn't taking this seriously. He didn't think this was funny. He said, "You have just earned yourself another 25 demerits. Also, it seems to me like you're going backward instead of forward."

I think I said something like, "Thank you for the profound insight." He said, "That's ten more demerits."

The social worker at the end of the table said, "I would like to see Darryl Wheat on a weekly basis. Does this committee object in any way?" No one did.

In less than four weeks, I had received no merits and had accumulated 75 demerits. At this rate, I was going to reach retirement age before being released from the Louisiana Training Institute.

Age:14
Location: Louisiana Training
Institute

# The Walking boss
# from hell...

The tradition at L.T.I. is that after you eat breakfast you go outside to the concrete slab at the front of the Institution to line up for whichever crew you're supposed to be on. Everyone is supposed to line up shoulder to shoulder and stand there for whatever amount of time it takes for instruction to be given. Each crew boss had his own designated area. Behind them in the grass would be kids that went to school or helped in the administration building or barn and so forth. So there were rows of boys who were supposed to keep total silence until they were released for the day.

As I arrived at the front, Mr. Walker (the boss of the punishment crew) said, "Wheat, fall in with my crew. You won't be running anywhere while you're on my crew."

I stated, "If it hadn't been for you, I wouldn't have run in the first place." Every boy in line froze and their eyes widened. I had apparently committed the unpardonable sin. Not one kid so much as breathed.

Walker walked over to me and stood in front of me. He said, "Oh, we have a talker. We'll just have to work that out when we get out on the crew line, won't we?"

Second mistake. I looked him straight in the face and said, "Whatever."

We loaded into Walker's truck to drive to the day's work. Walker's crew was usually made up of about ten boys and considered to be "the bad bunch" on campus. The most horrible, challenging jobs were for the Walker crew...cornfields, cleaning the swamps, cutting wet grass along the road that led to gullies full of snakes. It could have been likened to being on a chain gang. Walker seemed to have no conscience and certainly no consideration or empathy for children.

That day's goal was to retrieve a road that the swamp had taken over. We cut down most trees and made it travel-worthy again, watching out for alligators and snakes. One boy who had been on the crew for a considerable length of time cut his thumb off with a machete and was sent to the hospital. The boy next to me said it wasn't by accident, he did it on purpose, that he preferred to be in the hospital rather than on Walker's crew and the beatings that came with it. The kid looked around and then looked back and said, "You're probably going to get beat today for what you said in front of all the other boys and crew chiefs this morning. Walker is mean. They know what he does and they don't keep him from doing it."

The morning break could not have come too soon. Like the others, my jeans were soaked from the waist down from being in the swamp and I was wringing wet with sweat from the waist up. Walker passed the bucket of water past each boy. When he got to me, he hit the cup and spilled about half of the water. He looked at me and said, "Oops, I just spilled half of your water."

I just looked at him and didn't say a word.

He said, "You're being a good

**Dear Nanny,**

*...A boy cut off his thumb today. One just sat down in the rain and ate his muddy sock and is now being transferred to the State Mental Institution. Did he do the right thing? Is the current of shock treatment anymore detrimental than the electrodes of deprivation? Is the straight jacket any more confining than the regimentation here? Are the nights of irrational screams of the insane easier on the ear than the sobs of fear and anguish of scared children? I miss you.*

*D*

*It's not important how many guards are cruel or hateful, and we know that they are, but it is important what you think, believe and become that matters. Remain tough.*

**Love, Nanny**

boy. You won't run from my crew." My first thought was, *You're dreaming.* At lunch, my food tray was "accidentally spilled" on the roadway that we were clearing.

Walker said, "Excuse me. If you pick up the sandwich from the highway, you're welcome to put it back together."

I still had one piece of bread and some lettuce caught on it with the mayonnaise and I ate it. I didn't say anything but he just looked at me and smiled.

Out of his view, one of the boys walked by and handed me a tin cup of water, about three ounces. He said, "Drink it quickly and hand it back to me." I drank quickly and handed it back to him. The water tasted good.

At the end of the day, the truck was loaded with everyone except me. "Wheat, you sit up here in the front with me, Mr. Runaway."

These kinds of actions between the two of us continued for about a week or more. After that, I went up one morning to the front. Mr. Austin pushed me back into the second line, which would have been lining up for his crew. There were hardly ever any fights on his crew. I found out how lucky I had been when one kid said, "He just chose you."

I said, "He chose me?"

"Yeah. Austin can pick the kids he wants on his crew or send them back to Walker's crew or any other crew."

I asked the kid, "Why did he pick me? There are at least ten crews in this institution."

He said, "I think Mr. Austin likes you. Also, there are several boys from Baton Rouge on his crew and they all respect Mr. Austin. So will you."

So I was now on Austin's crew.

But nothing is private in a correctional facility and I was called into the social worker's office. I had been writing Nanny almost daily keeping her filled in on what was going on in my life. There was a rubber band around all of the letters that I had written sitting on the social worker's desk. The letters, according to their guidelines, were too revealing and, I was told, would not be sent if I reported everything that happened inside the Institution. I was informed that I could talk about myself, anything about myself, but no names could be contained in these messages. "You can say what we ate at a meal but you can't describe how bad the food is. You can't put in there who ran away or what people did because those are correctional secrets. If it's positive or neutral, you can say it. Otherwise, it's not allowed."

*Believe me, I will find a way to get around the rule and get my letters to Nanny!*

Reform schools are not a place you take for granted. You have to learn who you can trust and who you can't trust. You need to be aware that at any given moment any violent thing can happen to anyone. That included me. There were people coming into E Cottage from Baton Rouge. We had each other's back. Nevertheless, that wouldn't necessarily keep someone from quickly cutting you or stabbing you or hitting you in the head with a bottle regardless of the consequences to them. Therefore, your life was very vigilant, usually tense and you took nothing for granted. You live daily with some degree of fear and some degree of defense. You never wanted to leave yourself vulnerable.

In the mornings, you had to tie your bunk sheet as tight as you could and the kid designed to be "in charge of the bunks being all made up" let the guard know that the cottage was ready to go downstairs, get dressed, and line up for breakfast. However, the kid that was put in charge of the morning inspection had a lot of power. He's the one who made that decision and he could make some boy redo his bed as many times as he wanted. In fact, he could cause the whole cottage to miss breakfast, which in turn would result in consequences for the boy who caused everyone not to have their meal.

On weekends, the residents of each cottage went out in front of their own building and were not allowed to go far. We were playing a little softball and I cut my foot very badly on a broken Coke bottle. From under my toe, all the way to the back of my heel, it was split open.

Mr. Henderson, the walking boss, was in charge of taking kids to the hospital. He was called to take me to the hospital. As we left out the gates, instead of taking me to the downtown hospital, he took a left and took me to a very small clinic way outside the limits of town. My foot was cut badly and I was losing blood at a fast rate. When we arrived at the clinic, I was told to sit in the waiting room while he went and informed the doctor that I was there. I was bleeding pretty strongly and it was beginning to pool up around me on the floor. Henderson looked through a couple of doors in the waiting room and found a mop, shoved me off the chair onto the floor and told me to clean up the blood. I tried to mop it up but I was bleeding faster than I could mop it up and was having to stand on one foot. He hit me from behind and knocked me down saying, "I said clean it up."

I was sitting on the floor in my blood feeling faint. An Oriental couple had entered the waiting room and observed what was going on between me and Henderson. The man got up and left out the door. He apparently called the city police. An officer entered, saw the blood all over me, saw my foot still bleeding and asked Mr. Henderson, "They said you were beating a kid in the waiting room." It was obvious I was the kid because of the blood all over my clothes.

The Oriental man said, "That man there was beating the boy."

Henderson told the policeman, like it was no big deal, "That boy happens to be a bad inmate from the training school not far from here. He's defiant and nothing but trouble."

The policeman looked at me and the amount of blood and the horrifying look on the Oriental man's wife's face. He said to Mr. Henderson, "Maybe he's too hurt to clean it up."

Mr. Henderson told the officer that he would get the situation under control and be out of there shortly. While they were talking, I darted past the reception desk and found the doctor in one of the treatment rooms. I said, "Whatever you do on the face of the earth, you give me a handful of antibiotics or penicillin or something. I'll put them in my pocket." I put my foot on the gurney and asked him would he take the stapler and put my foot together as quick as he could. I told him, "That man in there is going to take me out of here without being treated."

The doctor remained calm but stated, "That will hurt bad. You need a pain killer and I need to clean it out."

Maybe it was the way that I looked at the doctor. "You don't have time. Hurry. That man will let me die. He doesn't care."

Reacting to the urgency in my voice, the doctor poured some water over the cut and reached for the stapler. He said, "This is going to hurt."

I said, "Don't worry about it. Just staple it, please."

The doctor handed me the bottle and I filled my pocket full of penicillin tablets and put my bloody sock back on. The officer walked into the examining room and said, "Are you okay?"

I said, "Yes, sir. Everything is fine." Henderson was standing at the door and I knew not to say anything more.

The police drove off and Henderson said, "Get in the car. You've gotten all the treatment you're going to get. You're going to learn how to get along here yet."

He took me through the gates to E Cottage, walked me to the door, unlocked the door, and said, "Now, walk up the stairs."

It was hard to do since I had to limp up the stairs and what I was wearing was full of blood. He wouldn't even let me wash my hands or change clothes.

The following day I had a noticeable limp and could barely walk. I made it all the way to the front to fall in but Mr. Austin pointed to his crew. After everyone fell out, he took me to a water faucet where I removed the bloody sock that was still there from the day before. He inspected the staples as best he could and handed me a rag to wash my foot and leg. The crew was raking leaves that day. He said, "I want you to take this rake and only rake near the base of this tree, and when I tell you to sit down, sit down and relax." The next day, he brought Band-aids, adhesive tape, and antibiotics from his own house. I knew he wasn't supposed to do that but, then again, Mr. Austin wasn't like other people.

Thank God I was on Mr. Austin's crew. I don't know how I would have gotten well otherwise. For a few days, I walked with a noticeable limp but his bandages and my penicillin was working.

## Nighttime...

I was still witnessing the same sad activities:children awake crying, children asleep crying, nightmares, screams, and sporadic acts of aggression from one person to another. My bunk still faced the bathroom and Red kept on with the oral sex with the boy that was smaller than him. I had had enough. I got up and walked in the bathroom and, before anything started, I grabbed Red by the hair on each side of his head and banged his face into the wall until he went limp. He was falling over the top of the commode and I added about five fist licks as he went down. The small boy looked at me and said, "Hey, man, thanks. Any time you need anything you just let me know."

The guard slept in the middle of the hallway on the second floor so no one could sneak out past him. After I had beat Red's face against the wall, he crawled to the guard and woke him up. He needed to go to the hospital. Apparently, he was cut over his eyes and had a broken nose and one of his teeth was knocked out. Of course, they called Henderson to take him to the hospital. A few days later, he returned from the hospital. Red didn't say anything to me, but he didn't mess with the little boy again.

Unbelievable. He ratted on me to the cottage parent and I was going to be reassigned to Walker's crew. It was time for me to take my second vacation from L.T.I. After one day on Walker's crew, a mattress from a vacant bunk was dropped out of a window for me to drape over the barbed wire of the fence and I took off. I made it to a truck stop where I found a truck driver who was headed for New Orleans. Before I escaped, another inmate had advised me that he had a female cousin who was a stripper who lived right off Canal Street, first place on the right-hand side. If I made it to New Orleans, I was to get to there and ask for Linda.

Some ten hours later, I arrived. Got out of the truck, crossed over the streetcar tracks, hit Bourbon Street, walked inside the described building and asked for Linda. Linda was there and surprised. "Oh, my goodness," she said. "That's my little cousin who told you about me. You can stay at my place tonight but, for right now, here's five dollars to get you some food."

My night on Linda's patio had been pleasant enough but she had left early for work the next morning. I started across the street to try to wrangle something to eat but was quickly surrounded by police cars. They put handcuffs on me and took me to the local precinct on Rampart Street. I was booked for correctional escape. I did not give them my real name but it wouldn't take them long before they found out who I was.

I spent the night figuring how to get out. I was on the first floor in jail cell number three. In the morning, after a biscuit and some scrambled eggs, they let us go out in the middle of the cell yard to get some exercise. I asked the guard who was in cell number one. He said, "Williams. Why?"

I said something to throw him off like, *I think he's kin to me.*

As I entered the yard where a basketball game was going on, I said, "Hey, is there anyone named Williams here?"

And one guy said, "Yeah, me."

I said, "The guard said we're supposed to change cells. I'm supposed to be in cell number one and you're supposed to be in cell number three. I'm supposed to see the judge in the morning right off to be transferred so he wants me to be first."

Williams said, "Okay."

Once back inside, the switch was made and the cell doors were locked.

An officer came to cell number one in the morning. "Are you Williams?" I said, "Yes, sir."

He said, "You're booked for drunk and disorderly. You have seven days to report to court."

So I signed my name 'Williams,' and went down the stairs and back to Linda's apartment. She gave me something to eat and a bunch of one-dollar bills to eat on during the day. I walked around the corner on Royal Street to a bookstore and picked up a used copy of Thomas Wolfe's "You Can't Go Home Again." I went back to Linda's apartment, the only place I knew to hide, knocked on the door, and her boyfriend answered. "Come in."

I said, "Okay." As soon as I walked in, I saw that a number of police officers were waiting for me. I was transferred back to New Orleans Parish jail on Rampart Street. I was picked up by one of the employees of L.T.I. and one of the state people hired to transport criminals. I was back on my way to L.T.I. with the second escape added to my record, more demerits and, of course, back on Walker's crew.

Walker and Henderson took turns for the next few weeks beating me up or looking the other way as fights occurred that involved me. I finally worked my way off of his crew. As I left, he said, "We'll break you down sooner or later."

I turned around and said, "Don't bet your whole pay-check on it."

Around this time, Baton Rouge friends were beginning to show up at the facility on a regular basis. All the ones that I had hung around with came. Up until now, the New Orleans area had had an overwhelming number of residents at the Institute and, therefore, wielded a great amount of power over who did what to whom and what the repercussions or consequences were. The Baton Rouge boys had been fierce fighters back home and the Institution was shocked as the Baton Rouge boys started showing up. Several of the people I had hung with were not there, but at least 10 to 12 were.

*"Stand tall. Never give up. Greatness can only come from courage."*

**Nanny**

The winter months came on and it was cold.

Few articles of clothing were supplied by the State and were distributed from only one locker room, not much larger than a closet. Mostly khaki-type pants and shirts. I remember working in the woods one day cutting trees and there was so much sleet and ice that there was ice all in my hair. I had some light-weight gloves and so at lunchtime, we made a fire and I sat down. I was warming my hand when one guy grabbed me and pulled me back. I had burnt the glove off my hand but I never felt it because my hands were that cold.

During that time, because of my second runaway, I was on Walker's crew and we had been working in the woods cutting trees while it was sleeting. It was very hard to get enough clothing on to make up for the fact that I didn't have a jacket. Jackets were hard to come by.

At the end of November, everyone was talking about being able to go home for a Christmas visit. I was excited about the possibility.

In late November, I was transferred back to Mr. Austin's crew. Our job was to prepare chickens for the institution's supper. That meant cutting off the heads and feet and plucking off the feathers and gutting the chickens. About ten kids were gathered around about a seven-foot table with enough 12-inch butcher knives for everyone to have one. I guess something was bound to happen, and it did. A sexual remark came from one knife-wielding kid standing next to me and the remark was apparently aimed at me. When no answer came, he said, "Hey, blondie, I'm talking to you."

Mr. Austin was standing outside but there was a guard sitting in the room with us looking out a window and not paying attention to what was going on. And apparently, that guard didn't want to have anything to do with what he assumed was about to happen. He knew that all the kids were holding butcher knives that they knew how to use and there was no way he could not have heard the comment to me from this kid. Everyone standing there in our group knew what was about to happen because every last one of them looked to the floor and backed away from the table. They wanted to be able to say they hadn't seen what was about to go down. That left me and the boy standing next to me at the table.

He took a whole chicken and hit me in the head with it. When I turned around and faced the guy who had hit me in the head with the chicken, he had a completely horrified look on his face. I honestly don't remember much at the moment, but I had taken my butcher knife and, in one quick motion, stabbed him through his leather jacket, through his left arm, and into his left side. When I looked down, the point of the knife blade was sticking out of the middle of his chest. I pulled the knife back out and put it to his throat and stated, "If you ever rat on me, believe this, I'm not going to stay here until I'm 21." (At the time I was 14.) I knew I had stabbed him badly and I realized that they could hold that charge over until I reached the age of 21, legal adult, and sentence me to Angola.

Mr. Austin was outside and obviously heard what was going on and came back inside. An ambulance was sent for the kid and Mr. Austin stayed with him until it arrived. Everyone returned to the butcher block table but no one was saying a word. Dead silence.

Mr. Austin returned back inside. He observed the kids' expressions and told them to get back to work. I felt Mr. Austin standing beside me. He said, "Are you okay?"

I said, "Yes, sir."

He said, "The boy says he fell on a knife. Does anybody here have a different story?"

None of the children spoke.

I'm sure Mr. Austin knew that I had done it. He knew the other kid was a troublemaker and he knew that I already had an ungodly reputation for protecting myself. He said, "Okay. Everybody go back to work."

The boy never told the administration on me. That doesn't mean that the population didn't know. In fact, I think every kid in the institution knew…rather quickly.

# Age: 14
# Location: Louisiana Training Institute

## The violent life of L.T.I...

I guess the realization I had stabbed another kid was a shock, even to me. I didn't remember the act of stabbing him at all. I guess the tension, the terror, his aggression must have made me snap as well as seeing the butcher knife in his hand and absolutely no support system. When you're in a correctional facility, either you protect yourself at all costs or you pay the consequences. Your act of aggression to protect yourself changes you. You do things that are violent and suffer the punishment consequences or you receive the acts of violence from other inmates. Big problem. That lack of respect for you ends up with people taking advantage of you across the institution in every situation.

Neither Mr. Austin nor any of the crew members mentioned the incident after it happened. The usual result of my act would typically and eventually result in a future retaliation. Actually, it didn't come from the stabbing victim but from one of his friends from another cottage.

The following week, while E Cottage was in the cafeteria line moving slowly and the food trays were being filled by inmates who worked as servers in the kitchen, I observed everyone ahead of me receiving a couple of large ladles full of pork and beans for this meal. When I arrived in front of the server to receive my portion, he gave me, not ladles full, but only three beans that he had carefully scooped into his serving spoon. I recognized him as a friend of the guy who I had stabbed. There was a smirk on his face and a challenging look. The serving bar was only about 30 inches wide and, without thinking or processing it, I scooped up a handful of the scalding hot beans on the serving line between us and threw it in his face. He screamed and grabbed his face, which was full of beans and gravy dripping down. Guards, of course, came from all directions.

A handkerchief was quickly thrust into my hand by the guy in front of me and the guy in back of me was tearing off part of his t-shirt. Both of them said, "Hurry up and wipe your hands off," and they kicked the rags under the serving bar. No one ratted on me and the guards took the injured server to the hospital. Again, that didn't mean that the word didn't spread quickly across the inmates as to who did what to whom. Word travels through an institution like lightning.

E Cottage had been designated for some of the most defiant and unruly kids. While E Cottage inmates lived up to their reputation, they also received the most mean and cruel guards.

Three Sundays out of every month were designated as a potential visiting day for families, of course, scheduled in advance through the administration. The fourth

Sunday offered an extremely different kind of entertainment—forced fighting. For the guards' amusement, names of each cottage member were put in a hat and two pieces of paper were drawn so that they could go to the middle part of the cottage and fight each other. It was horrible and totally insane. The fights were fierce and bloody, each person afraid to get hurt by the other person. My greatest fear was that I would be paired off with a person who might be a weaker fighter or someone I liked. It happened. The other name that was drawn was a guy who happened to be a friend. I could beat him and fight him

*...I don't understand these people. What are they trying to do to us? What's the point of changing all of a person? It's as though they feel we walked through the gates with no personality at all. What's worse is that if they feel like we're just like clay to be molded, they are creating grotesque sculptures you couldn't even give away at a flea market. Who is responsible for this modern day funeral?*

***Darryl***

*Never give up. Learn to love yourself. Stand in the heavens... for I believe the angels have a great assignment for you.*

***Nanny***

and he would do his best to hold his own and somebody would get hurt for no damned reason whatsoever except for the pleasure of the guards.

The kid was my size, but he was "solid" and I was disgusted with the whole institutional process. We walked to the middle of the room. The inmates were mildly frustrated because they knew we were friends, but my friend put his fist up. I put my hands on his shoulders and kissed his forehead and walked back to my seat. The guard was near me and screamed at me, "What are you doing?"

I said, "I'm not hitting him."

As usual, the cottage was speechless when I frequently did something bizarre or considered to be out of context in reform school. The guard was also shocked. He looked at me like, I don't believe what you just did.

The guard screamed in my face, "You will pay for that."

The whole cottage was listening for what I would say. I said, "I have no doubt. Nevertheless, I care more about his feelings and welfare than I do yours."

The guard advanced on me and said, "Don't you sass me." He hit me about three times. You could hear a pin drop in the cottage.

I said, "Wouldn't it be interesting if some of the guards pulled their own names out of the hat to fight some of the inmates in E Cottage?"

He had a small hammer handle in his back pocket that he used to hit me.

The last couple of days in November, I was called to the administration building and told I was being transported back to Baton Rouge for a "visit." That was odd and surprising. The next day, I showed up at my house with Nanny. Baton Rouge Junior High School was open, so I visited some of my old friends who hadn't been to L.T.I. yet. I told them not to come, that it wasn't what they expected.

That afternoon, back at Nanny's house, a phone call interrupted a conversation she and I were having. The phone call was obviously serious. She ushered me out of my grandfather's hearing and said the parole officer told her I would be going to court in the morning. Then she asked me about the white marks on both of my arms and the back of my hands and also the backs of my arms. She asked me how I got them. I told her that the guards put their cigarettes out on me. I estimated that there were about 40 white scars in various places on both of my arms. She took a deep breath, stood up, kissed me on my forehead, and said, "That's unacceptable," and went out on the back porch.

The next morning, the parole officer picked me up and took me before the judge at my hearing. I was informed that the wording of my sentence was being changed from what it had been when I was sent to L.T.I. When you're sent to L.T.I., the sentence is usually serving eight to nine months or acquiring 100 merits. I was informed that my sentence was going to be changed now to an indefinite sentence. I really didn't know what that meant, but okay. Not until I returned to L.T.I. did I learn what indefinite sentence really meant. It meant that both the judge and the institution had to agree on my parole for me to be released. It dawned on me, at my current age of 14, I could be looking at up to seven more years, in other words, the age of 21, before being released from that crazy place. I had a pretty lousy reputation with the administration.

I returned back to E Cottage and was informed that approximately 25 children in the institution would not be allowed to go home for Christmas. Of course, I was one of them. All the kids not allowed to go home moved into E Cottage. Some were 18 years old, 19 years old. Some were 190 pounds. Some were 6'3". Some were serving their second sentence. It was a tough crowd. On the second day, one of the larger kids from another cottage said, "You have quite a reputation for being so little, but one of these days someone is really going to hurt you."

I said, "I don't doubt it," and I didn't know whether that comment was a statement of fact or a threat, so I hit him about four times and knocked him down. It wasn't my only fight during the Christmas holiday with guys from other cottages but I was put in solitary confinement for this one.

Christmas did have a highlight. I was able to call and talk with Nanny and my mother. They were all gathered to celebrate at Nanny's house. Each of us was allowed a three-minute phone call.

"Are you okay?"

I said, "Great. Everything is okay."

My grandmother knew that I was not telling the truth. I had snuck out a number of letters telling her the truth about this place and what I was going through and the changes that were happening to me and the insanity and cruelty that I was observing. When she got on the phone, she said, "How are you really?"

I said, "This place is a den of hell. And to think the population has voted and paid their taxes to put us here to learn how to be a criminal and an outsider for life. I'm doing the best I can to get through," I told her. I said things that I wasn't able to put into a letter.

Another interesting happening…on Christmas day. There was a chapel on the campus near the dining hall, but it was mainly for show. No formal church events were ever held in that building. I broke line and opened the door. I turned the lights on and walked to the stage where there was a podium with a Bible on it. The door remained open and I started reading loud enough to be heard. You don't grow up in Nanny's house without knowing the first four books in the New Testament by heart, especially Jesus' words. I started reading some of Jesus' quotes, then turned to the Sermon on the Mount, explaining what Jesus meant as I read. Kids started gradually filing in. The guards didn't stop them. I think they were conflicted over the positive spiritual happening and the fact that we had broken line.

Kids sifted in from the various cottage lines. They sat down and listened, seriously. You can't hear Jesus' words without knowing that someone loves you and is pulling for you. There was no noise whatsoever. About ten minutes later I finished reading. The kids were all staring at me. Several thoughts went through my head as I looked at the other kids. *Can you believe that we're all here?* I thought that and then said it out loud. "Can you believe that we don't know what our future is, that our lives will never be the same after being here? And can you believe that someone lived that believes in the goodness of each one of us and is pulling for us?" Nobody said anything. I closed the Bible, walked outside. The boys followed and everybody went back to their own cottages without comment; not even from the guards. It was peaceful.

> *Dear Nanny,*
> *I feel like I'm looking through a microscope at the secret soul of man. I have seen the good and the bad, witnessed his most secret instincts.*
> *I can never be a child again.*
>
> **Darryl**

I was thinking to myself this cottage is full of people being punished for the behavior they need help with. According to statistics, most who leave here will go on to the state penitentiary, get shot, possibly killed, go to jail, become alcoholics, become violent. I thought about all the kids who had come to L.T.I. at that moment and how insane, cruel, strange this situation was and how the general population had permitted and supported its existence. Great schooling! They learned the best way to break into cars, how to burglarize businesses, how to steal and sell stolen goods, how to forge checks. It felt sad.

What's strange is, I guess, I never wanted to hurt anybody. I never stole a woman's purse or took anything from someone poor or vulnerable. It would have never dawned on me to hold up a frightened family or to hold someone hostage. I didn't feel like a criminal but that's what the institution taught me. That's what my current peers knew how to do. Ultimately, as people get older, their reputations are ruined for work, they're abandoned by their families. They're angry, fearful. Do all the wrong social things. Females resort to compromise to feed their young. Men disrespect their parents and neglect their children. L.T.I. was a college. You learned how to be a criminal in here. The recidivism rate was around 98%.

I had accumulated somewhere between 150 and 175 demerits, and of course, you needed 100 positive merits to get out. After Christmas, I was called to the administration building and I was informed that I was to be tested by a psychologist. I was given a test that centered on sensitive questions about my mother, my father, my home life, how I had been treated, trust issues, and so on. The questions stopped me in my tracks. I had about six pencils. I broke each of the pencils into about three pieces and walked into the psychologist's office and sprinkled them over his head. The test was ripped up in front of him and I sprinkled all the pieces over him.

A couple of days later, I was called in front of the disciplinary committee. I was sure my mountain of demerits was going to get higher, so I was quite surprised when the psychologist told them he would not agree to that and he would not sign the report. The head of the demerit committee argued with him, but the psychologist wouldn't do it and walked out, got into his car and left. I was told that even though I didn't get any demerits that I was getting assigned to Walker's crew—the detention crew. That's because it was cold, sleeting, raining and there was no way to get enough clothes to protect you from the cold.

The social worker scheduled me to come in the day after. She asked me why I did what I did and I told her about the questions involving my mother, my daddy, my family, and that I couldn't take it. I just wanted to quit. She said, "I'd like to see you more often."

I said, "You're one of about three people around here who's nice, so thank you for your concern. But once you walk out of the administration building, it's a jungle out there and talking in here doesn't change what's out there. Out there should fit what's in here when we're talking and it doesn't."

The correction boss, Mr. Henderson, who went from crew to crew and checked to make sure that there were no fights or issues, made sure to come around and make it known how he really felt about me. He passed the word on to Walker and any assistants to keep an eye on me because of my history of defiance, running away, and that "too many children thought too much of me."

But Henderson wasn't the only person who had me on their list. Tucker, a college student and guard, was an authority figure on campus and I had somehow managed to be a person of interest for him for about six months. He was a graduate student and he exuded the love of power and the hate of kids. It was about late January and I had done something wrong, and he pulled me to one side and told me that I was going to apologize to him in front of the whole cottage. Command was reinforced roughly by squeezing my genitals about three times and choking me. We walked to the middle of the room in E Cottage and everyone stopped doing what they were doing. Everybody was quiet. I stated, "I am supposed to apologize to everyone in E Cottage for Tucker, the guard, being a son of a bitch."

Eyes widened all around the room, even Tucker's. I went and sat down. He just stood there. He said, "You'll pay for that."

Indeed. He was able to get me back on several occasions. On one occasion, I was winning a fight with a boy who was about six to seven inches taller than me and outweighed me by about 100 pounds and Tucker walked up and hit me on the back of my head with a pipe, giving the guy time enough to get up and land some nice blows on my face.

It was in early spring, probably the middle of March, when I was approached by the coach and told that I was going to play baseball. He had heard all about me and my Little League baseball success. I told him, "No, I'm not going to play baseball."

He said, "Oh, yeah. You're playing baseball."

Although he was about 6'4", I looked at him and said, "No, I won't."

He said, "Listen to me. You're either going to play baseball or I will make sure your life is a nightmare."

I actually laughed and said, "What do you call what I'm living now?

This isn't a nightmare being here?"

It was in late January because rumors started that there was a group coming to the facility to investigate how the place was running and if there were any abusive situations. The barbed wire on the front and back gates had been removed prior to their arrival.

I know this sounds crazy, but it's hard for me not to believe that my grandmother called my uncle, who was the advertising editor of the Baton Rouge paper and had some pull and talked to him about the conditions of L.T.I. and persuaded him to react in some manner. As

I said, I know it sounds crazy but it certainly sounds like something that Nanny would do.

These official-looking people left. None of us knew what their credentials were or who they worked for but they interviewed numerous kids and staff. However, strange things happened after their departure. Mr. Moody, the house parent, called me in to sit near him to have a private conversation. He said, "You're going to be the count-off person for E Cottage. Also, for all extracurricular activities, such as playing baseball, you'll get extra credits. And you're going to be in charge of checking the beds. Also, you're scheduled to go in front of the demerit committee this week."

I said, "What for?"

He said, "Discuss it with them."

I was stunned. I said, "What do you mean?" I couldn't believe I was being put in control of these activities. I did know that these responsibilities carried an extra amount of merits against my substantial total of demerits. On the other hand, having an indefinite sentence, would these merits even matter and correlate and would L.T.I.'s perception of me correlate with the judge's opinion and result in a possible parole?

Age: 15
Location: Louisiana Training
Institute and "Home"

12

## Some New Transitions...

Sometime later in January, several serious things happened. I'll start with the first one. I was called to the demerit committee in the administration building. I was told that the runaway was going to be reduced in terms of amounts, two fights were going to be forgiven, and, when it was all over, I think over 100 demerits had been forgiven. At that point, I think I may have just barely had a minus column. And, with all the new duties at E Cottage, next month I should be in the positive range. Things like this never happened at L.T.I. So who was responsible for this, our Creator or Nanny or both?

The next thing that happened in January was that instead of Baton Rouge boys trickling in, as they had in November, December, and January, about 15 boys from Baton Rouge came in at one time. Most were unafraid of a fight and all of a sudden the kids from New Orleans seemed to take second place.

> *"You can't beat someone who refuses to give up."*
>
> **Nanny**

It turned out that I did play baseball after all even though I had refused at first. I heard how the team would travel to different states. That made it more interesting. The coach put me back on the mound as a pitcher but it's difficult to say that we had a strong baseball team for our age group.

I took the mound, in early February and he started putting up hitters. They couldn't hit curves, drops, sliders, or my fastball. The coach walked out to the mound, took my hand and bent it just about to the breaking point and said, "I need you to throw the ball where the batters can hit it."

I did what he asked. I needed a catcher, so I requested someone who I knew had played Little League baseball. The coach said, "He has a runaway history. It's his second time here and I can't trust the two of you together."

As I could, I said, "Then I'm not pitching." He asked me, "Why him?"

I said, "Because he actually can fill the position as my catcher. Without that, what's the use of having a pitcher? And the kid can hit, too."

So my choice was honored the following afternoon in practice and I stayed with the team.

A day or two later, I was called to the demerit committee and told that I was in the positive range, probably because I had extra merits for the E Cottage duties. And I should explain along with these duties, out of the 50 boys in the cottage at least 20 of them didn't like me correcting them or forcing them to redo their bed or to count off a second time. So with the gold, you also got some rust. Remember, it's a correctional institute. What had I expected?

We went and played two games in Arkansas. There was a second pitcher on the team. About halfway through the game, they knocked him out of the box and I finished the game. The following day, I was to pitch all of the second game. The kids from Arkansas seemed to have had more of a history of playing baseball than our boys.

The cleanup hitter (the person who bats fourth in the lineup) took the plate, mouthed off to me that just because I had experience didn't mean he wasn't going to knock the next ball out of the park. He said, "Throw it, you punk!"

Both teams heard him, so the next ball was a fastball, which landed in his left ribs as hard as I could throw it. He hit the ground. Both coaches knew I had done it on purpose. *So what?*

While my coach liked to win, this didn't go over so good. He came out to the mound, looked me in the eye and said, "Enough. I'll deal with you later."

Incidentally, we won both games.

We went from Arkansas to Mississippi and played two games there. We won both games, but they also had played baseball before and played us hard. However, the kids were likeable and would shake hands with us after the game.

I might mention that the coach had begun to dictate what pitches he wanted me to pitch, in particular constantly throwing curveballs. It was causing a lot of pain in my arm and shoulder and a lot of swelling in my wrist after the games. This was getting worse and I was getting angry. I made the coach aware of the pain from throwing these same pitches, but his statement was, "These trips are costing the Institute money and we have to have some more wins in order to justify it."

Our schedule took us from Mississippi into Florida and our first stop was in Pensacola. The coaches were going to let us go swimming. Near the beach was a beautiful speed boat. I signaled to my baseball catcher and friend to jump in or, in other words, let's run away. Problem…the boat stalled about 40 feet away from shore and the evening tide kept it from going out or coming in. I couldn't start the boat. People on the beach gathered. Our team gathered. The coach had to call the Coast Guard to come pull the boat in. Needless to say, the coach wasn't happy. And neither was the owner, who had watched the whole fiasco from the shore.

After the beach incident, my assigned seat was at the front of the bus where I was handcuffed to the railing in front of me. Our next stop as we made our way through the state was in a town that had caverns. We were going to take a tour to see stalactites and stalagmites. Again, I saw this as a great opportunity to run away. Again, the team catcher was with me for the second runaway attempt in two days. With the same great success that we had with the boat, we got lost in the caverns and had to holler for help. I tried to explain to the coach that, while I loved baseball, I didn't love being at L.T.I. Of course, punishments were doled out.

We finally made it to Marianna, Florida, to play their reform school. After the two runaway incidents, the coach lectured us about making fools of ourselves and Louisiana Training Institute. I raised my hand.

And he said, "What?"

I asked, "Do you think that's possible to make a reform school look any worse than it is?"

Anyway, two things happened in Florida that were interesting. One, the food was put in the middle of the table for the kids to eat as much as they wanted. That was a nice change. And the second, the kids were fun to play against. One of our hitter's fly balls backed up their center fielder all the way to the fence, over which he jumped and kept running. Both teams cracked up laughing. Strangely, none of the coaches did.

Our tour took us to Alabama next. After striking out, one of their best hitters threw his bat at me. In return, I hit him twice with two baseballs before he could make it to the dugout, which caused both teams to pour out onto the field. It took a while to calm both teams down and I was informed that I would be punished. While the rest of my team was allowed to bed down in the facility's basketball gym, I was ushered to the solitary confinement area.

There were two boys already in there and it looked more like a bedroom with a bathroom. One boy said to the other boy, "New meat. We're going to have some sex tonight."

He sat on the windowsill and we were on the second floor of the building. I acted like I was going to look out the window but, instead, hit him and knocked him through the glass and out the window. I broke a vase and came to the other guy. He backed away and kept saying, "Okay. Okay." He put his hands up and said, "Everything is cool. Count me out."

My coach and the Alabama administration people were trying to get through the door that I had locked from the inside. I still had the vase in my hand while the coach was banging on the door and mouthing, "No, no, no."

I yelled through the door, "I'll put it down when he apologizes." The kid immediately said, "Let it go. Everything is cool. I'm out."

My coach and their administrator, or guard or whatever, were able to open the door and come in and I was immediately handcuffed by my coach. He brought me down to where the rest of the team was and my night was spent on the gym floor next to my coach's bed with the handcuffs hooked under the left leg of his bunk. At some point during the night, I pried the coach's bed up to free my cuffs and went out the gym door to smoke a cigarette.

It took a while for the coach to wake up and realize that I was no longer restrained by his cot, or even in the building. He found me a short time later just outside the door where I was sitting. "Why didn't you run away?"

I said, "I don't know. I wasn't thinking about that at all."

Actually, while I had been alone for about an hour, my thoughts had kept me occupied. *What's going to happen in the future? How long will I stay in L.T.I.? How much correction and lack of freedom? How many more fights? I miss Baton Rouge. I miss home.*

But actually what hurt most was my missing Nanny. I missed talking to her, having breakfast and coffee with her. I missed her support and wisdom. And compassion. *The life I'm living is not the life I want for myself.*

I remember her saying in one of her last letters, "You can make it. You can do this. If you have to survive this, then you just do it. Don't change. Don't let others hurt you. But don't develop the habit of hurting yourself. Whatever is coming in your future, *Take whatever "they" have to dish out, but remain "yourself" and never be a coward because weakness has its own punishment. What things you have to do, remember where you are and the fact that His design is for you to survive in some healthy way.*

*Nanny*

133

there will be an end to this. One day you will make it. One day you'll be free."

That last statement reminded me of when I showed her the baseball I had received at the end of the 7th grade that had printed on it

"Best Little League Baseball Player." Nanny had taken a ballpoint pen and added something else: "Who will play on a greater team someday."

Age: 15
Location: Baton Rouge,
Louisiana

## How do you find freedom...

13

It was July 1957. We had left the Florida game on the way home and had reached Louisiana where it was extremely hot. July is always hot in Louisiana. I was fully aware that demerits were going to be added after the two attempted escapes while on our trip and all of the other issues that had occurred, but I found out that Coach had other plans. He refused to sign off on my being assessed any demerits and explained to the committee that whatever bad behavior had occurred on the trip had been taken care of. The committee did not overrule him on his decision.

And, after our return to the Institute, I started hearing rumors that my parole had come in. In other words, I had achieved 100 merits and wasn't currently facing any demerit charges. I made an appointment with the social worker who confirmed that my parole was actually in, but the look on her face indicated not all the news was good. I said, "So the parole is in and I can go home? When?"

And she said, "They're not releasing you yet from the L.T.I. system." She tried to comfort me by saying, "Don't get upset."

Boy, did I ever get upset! I told her she was a nice lady but I told her that she didn't have any power to do anything against this crazy place and that I had no respect for the administration. She tried to calm me down by saying she was sure I would get to go home soon.

I said, "I told you I had no control whether I came or went when we first talked. This is run more like a cruel children's penitentiary and has the audacity to call itself a training institute? It trained me all right...trained me not to trust people in charge of your life, people who worked for the justice system, people who worked for the correctional system, and it's no wonder that you leave this place worse than when you came. The people inside of this place don't care anything about you and the people outside of this place don't care what the people inside do to me."

I left the administration upset and walked across the square to E Cottage. An E Cottage inmate was standing near the Coke machine and I told him to grab a Coca-Cola bottle, to smash the cigarette machine and hand me a couple of packs of cigarettes.

On the other side of this little Coca-Cola canteen, Henderson had parked his car and was talking to a house parent. He heard the machine smash and walked around to see me standing there with the cigarettes. I told the boy that had broken open the machine, "Walk away," and told Henderson that I was the one who broke open the machine. I said, "I'll turn around and go back to the demerit committee."

He said, "No, you're going to get in the car with me."

I said, "Not this time, you moron."

He told me to stop or I would regret it. I said something like, "I already regret that you are alive."

He said, "You will-regret this."

I walked over to the demerit committee and said I just smashed the cigarette machine

*June 1957*

*Dear Nanny,*

*I'm slipping. Pray God tell me what kind of mad train I'm riding on... The heat is suffocating but I'm afraid of vomiting no matter how dizzy I get because I'm afraid my mind is going to come up with it. I have no head or brain, just some snarled up animal inside my bowels which could strike without warning or permission. How long can the human mind hold on to the ledge? How many times can acid go through the spinal canal till it laps over the lips and down the Shirt of Permanence?*

*D*

and stole some cigarettes out of it. They said they were closing the demerit committee for the day but the people who were still sitting at the table wrote down what I said. I shut the door and walked back to E Cottage.

At about 2:30 in the morning, I woke up to see Henderson standing over my bunk telling me to get up and come with him. He put handcuffs on me and took me to the barn. The barn was about 150 yards away from E Cottage behind the gym. He proceeded to wrap a towel around his hand and beat me half senseless. I tried to block some of his hits. I don't know why I didn't hit him back except for thinking that I'll never get out of here if I do. I must have lost consciousness because I came to a few hours later still in the barn and locked in a horse stall. I didn't know what time it was but I could hear and realized it was the person I knew who came every morning to attend and feed the animals in the barn.

I called out to him and he came around the outside of the building until we were on either side of the wall. He said he couldn't get me out because there was a lock on the gate. He told me of a rotting board that, if I kicked it hard enough, would probably break. I managed to break enough boards loose to be able to crawl my way out of the barn.

I realized my side hurt. It felt like Henderson had broken one of my ribs. I could feel dried blood around my mouth and nose and a cut over my eye. In fact, it seemed like there were small cuts all over my face. I could tell it was the time of the day when breakfast was over and all the boys were lining up to go back to their cottages. Painfully, I started a slow walk from the barn to the concrete area to fall in. Before long, I became the center of attention of everyone in the area. As I approached, boys were punching each other and there were whispers of, "Look, look. That's Wheat."

*There is no greater power than what is already in you. Don't forget to use it.*

**Nanny**

I walked all the way to the front where people go to fall in for the day's work. The boys had already started formation and I came up through the middle of the crews to take my place in the front. I drew the attention of each of the rows as I passed.

On the way there, I put my shirttail in. Mr. Swanson, the chief administrator of L.T.I., came out of the headquarters. He exchanged a look with Henderson who turned up his hands as if to say, "I screwed up" or "I forgot about him" or something. Henderson acted like he knew he was in trouble.

When I reached the front, Mr. Swanson was about 20 feet to my left and Henderson was about 20 feet to my right. The institution states you're supposed to have your shirttail tucked in when you fall in. A couple of boys supported me from either side because I was having trouble standing, but I wasn't through. I had something to say, loud enough for everybody to hear me. "My grandmother said that this is America and, if I want to wear my shirttail out, I can do it." I proceeded to take my shirttail out in front of the whole formation, Mr. Swanson and all of the crew leaders. I could see about 50 boys trying to hide their smiles while looking at the ground. For a while, no one moved. Mr. Henderson was waiting for Mr. Swanson to say something. He didn't. The crew members were waiting for what would happen next.

Walker broke the silence and called out, "Walker's crew, fall out." He named each boy as they passed to get on the truck.

As I turned, Mr. Austin said, "Wheat, fall out." No one said anything to me including Mr. Swanson or Mr. Henderson, even though everyone who had heard those three words knew what they meant. Mr. Austin had saved me from the detention crew. Mr. Swanson didn't say anything to stop it.

Mr. Austin's crew was supposed to be raking leaves that morning but, when we came to the first cottage, all I could do was lean against a tree. One kid came by and gave me a biscuit. Within minutes, another kid came by and handed me a Coca-Cola. Then a third kid came by and gave me a candy bar. The acid of the Coke burned my cut lips but the food was appreciated. I went to rake up some leaves and one boy pushed me back against the tree and said, "We got this."

I stayed on Austin's crew for the rest of the day. The kids let me have a rake in my hand but wouldn't let me do anything with it. Mr. Austin was well aware of the assistance I was receiving from the rest of the crew and obviously supported it. A pack of cigarettes landed in my pocket, a Coke in my hand every time one ran out, a biscuit or a peanut butter and bread sandwich each time I finished one. And that's how the day went.

About a week later, I was given the news that my parole had come in and I was being discharged. On a Saturday morning, an old city bus, used to transport kids, came around to pick me up to take me to the bus station. The Institute was to give each paroled inmate their bus ticket home. The bus driver opened the door. Mr. Moody, the house parent, had been the one to hand me my bus ticket and was sitting in the front yard about 15 feet to my left. The bus driver, after a few minutes of waiting for me to get on, finally said, "Are you coming or going?"

I said, "I don't need anything from L.T.I." I wadded up the ticket and threw it on the floor of the bus. He closed the door and drove off.

Mr. Moody broke the silence after the bus had left. I'll never forget what he said: "You'll be back in less than three months." He said, "You're the most violent, defiant, and intelligent child that I've ever had at E Cottage, maybe that I've ever had. But you'll be back in less than three months."

I turned around and looked at Mr. Moody. "That will be a scientific impossibility, not unless they bring me back in a coffin and drop me at E Cottage. I'll never come back here." With that and with the boys watching, I walked to the front gate, pushed it open, and walked to the highway.

Hard to believe, but one of the Baton Rouge E Cottage boys' parents had come to visit him and were leaving just then to go back home. They asked me where I was going and I said, "Back to Baton Rouge. My parole has come in."

They said, "Well, get in. We'll take you home." I took them up on their offer.

So many things churned through my mind. I was sitting in the back seat and the wind was blowing in my face and through my hair. They were supposed to be the winds of freedom but L.T.I. had done so many things to my personality. *Am I really free? Can the person they changed me into remain free? Will I be treated like I'm free? What is this parole thing about and what will they do to me? Will parole be just another set of handcuffs and chains? Will the parole officer be anxious to send me back?*

I was thinking in my mind how much I had changed over the years. Before and during my time at L.T.I., what had I learned about life, about people and their emotions, about crime, and fake helpers? I had come to the conclusion that everyday society doesn't care what happens to their children with problems and that certain institutions can change someone into an outsider that seemingly no longer belongs outside of barbed wire and restraints.

Yes, I had definitely changed and the big question was if I changed in some bad ways, could I change back?

I was "out" but realized I was very disconnected from everything that was going on and my trust of many things had been greatly diminished. I was aware that my inner self had been damaged and holes had been shot into it. I had remained strong and unbent through the institutional experience for the purpose of getting back home, to my back porch, to my life, my family, and my coffee with Nanny. I had resisted L.T.I. from changing me into something they wanted me to be and they had not succeeded in breaking me. But the resistance to that had also created a very different, non-trusting, aggressive, hyper-vigilant, even self-hating me.

At this moment now, life felt surreal.

My ride let me off at the corner of Plank Road and Washington Avenue, two blocks from mine and Nanny's house at 2755 Washington Avenue. I had to prepare my mind and take some deep breaths before walking the short distance to get to Nanny. With all that I had been through, what would it be like being home again, touching my grandmother again, being loved by my grandmother and grandfather? It was exciting but scary.

I arrived. I walked toward the backyard where Nanny was hanging clothes and I went straight up to her. She had that Nanny smile on her face like, *You did it, you're here.* I just put my arms around her. She put her chin on top of my head and quietly said, "Like I said before, I'm still behind you 100 percent regardless of what happens in either one of our lives."

She let go of me and smiled. Putting her head back, she said, "Would you like some coffee?"

Now, I was home. I said, "Absolutely."

Nanny and I were sitting on the front porch catching up and I was letting some of the tension flow out of my body when a police car with two officers showed up. They told me I would need to get in the car. I said, "Give me a good reason."

The officer showed me a piece of paper where it said I had been paroled to my mother at her house. The officer said, "This is where we're supposed to take you."

I asked him if he had lost his damn mind. I said, "I live here."

He said, "The judge paroled you to Fairfields Drive to your mother's house."

I said, "I'm not going. That's not my home." He said, "It's either there or jail."

So much for freedom. Freedom certainly doesn't know my name!

My mother greeted me at the door and showed me the paperwork proving what the officers had said. "Mother, this is not my house. I'm not going to do this. Call the court and change it."

Mother looked at me and said, "We will all try to get along together."

I couldn't believe this horror and turn of events. I hadn't been out of L.T.I. 24 hours; my life was going to hell. My stepfather still hated my guts and I had learned to hate his. Even though it was seven years earlier, I still had the vivid memory of the day they drove off and left me (abandoned me?) to live with my grandmother.

While Mother was showing me my room and the rest of the house, I was reeling with shock. I was devastated. First day, an absolute back-to-L.T.I. guarantee: This was never going to work.

My stepfather came home from work and his first words to me were at the supper table. "So you're out of jail."

I stopped eating and looked at him. "Actually, at this moment it doesn't feel that way. At this moment, it feels like I'm still in jail." He and I both knew that this wasn't going to work. He was mean and didn't like me and I had just spent the last year learning how to deal with people like him and, unfortunately for him, the aggression that accompanies it.

So, I guess I was supposed to just slip back into life like everything was okay and everything was going to be okay. The following weekend, my stepfather got me up early before breakfast or coffee and informed me about some of my new assignments. One was the huge task of refurbishing and painting the inside of their garage. Also, painting the outside of the house was high on the list of upcoming projects and, on my first weekend

145

there, I was supposed to mow the lawn. He informed me that I was supposed to mow the lawn each week.

Baton Rouge is my home and my heart, but at this time of year, the heat and humidity were always incredible. I asked him what he was going to do on the weekends if I was going to do all the work. He said, "You'll just do what I tell you. Remember, you're on parole."

That certainly had the same ring of all the L.T.I. guards. There wasn't any love lost between the two of us.

My instructions had been given and we understood each other. I started walking back to the house. He said, "Where are you going? You need to cut the yard."

A reminder: I hadn't had any breakfast or coffee. My first thought: *This is really different than Nanny's house where we always talked, ate, and had coffee together, then started our life.*

I started the lawnmower and started doing the back yard. Between the heat, the humidity, being hungry and the attitude of my stepfather, I just couldn't do it. At the back part of their lot, the lawn dipped about three feet down into a creek that always had water in it. The two-foot deep creek became the resting place for the lawnmower after I threw it in there. He was on his way outside as I was coming into the house. I looked at him and said, "Go to hell."

The second week began even worse. My stepfather and my mother had a late-night screaming match because he came in drunk at about midnight with lipstick all over his shirt. The raised voices woke me up and I entered the same room where they were to aim one of my comments at him. It was painful to see my mother in tears. He warned me to stay out of it. The argument died down and I went back to bed.

At some point during the night, and it seemed so surreal, I started being hit hard with something—someone's fist or a hammer handle or something. I blacked out at some point during the assault because I wasn't aware of anything again until the morning. I wanted to confront my stepfather but he had already left for work. However, I was ready for him when he came in that afternoon and blocked his path through the house. "I want to make you a promise and I give you my word. If anything else happens to me, I will respond. If you try to hurt me, you have my word I'll put you in the hospital."

My mother witnessed the confrontation and the threats he made afterward about reporting me to my parole officer and the police and "whipping" me if I kept on. I went into the room they had assigned to me and retrieved my uncle's M-1 from the war. I tried to put the clip in but I wasn't at all familiar with firearms. I cocked it and aimed it right at him, stating, "You will never, never, never whip me."

> *"Life is tough; you just have to be tougher."*
> **Nanny**

His complexion paled. He took a few steps back and went into the kitchen. I threw the M-1 onto the floor. The bullets came out. I must have put the bullets in wrong. I remember thinking, *I can't do anything right.*

From behind me, he picked up the gun and put it to my throat and choked me until I passed out. When I came to, my stepfather was gone and Mother was sitting a few feet away. "You're going to have to leave here."

I looked at her and replied, "You understand that if I leave here, according to the piece of paper that you have I'm going back to reform school."

She just said, "You're still going to have to leave here."

I couldn't believe what my mother had said. She had chosen him over me....again. I walked over to my grandmother's house and sat on the porch. My grandfather informed me that my stepfather had come by and said, "Your grandson has threatened to shoot me." My grandfather said, "You treated him like dirt when you were here. But to respond to your verbal report, if I were you since he threatened to shoot you, I'd leave."

I spent the night at my grandmother's house. I got a cup of coffee first thing the next morning and went out to the front porch where Nanny was talking to my parole officer. They stopped talking and I was invited me to sit down. The parole officer stated, "I'm allowing you to stay at your grandmother's house but I'm going to report that you're living with your mother and you're visiting your grandmother's house. I agree with your grandmother; this situation doesn't prove anything. There's no use for you to get out of L.T.I. and then turn around and go directly back."

I was seriously relieved. I was also shocked that somebody in the justice system had done something compassionate. I had not witnessed that in a long time. He patted me on the back, smiled and left. Nanny and I went inside and repeated the tradition that had started at age five—we drank some coffee, ate breakfast and talked.

Age: 15 - 16
Location: Baton Rouge,
Louisiana

# Back to the 10th grade
# – more than once...

So I guess I was supposed to slip back into my high school life the same way I was supposed to slip back into my family life. After registration and a couple of days of school had passed, the principal called me into his office.

"I just want you to know that I don't expect any trouble out of you. I've read the reports on you and I'm fully aware of the problems you've caused everywhere you've been, whether it's school, jail, home. And you're not going to cause any problems here. Do we understand each other?"

My answer to him was, "Does that include not committing armed robbery of the school cafeteria register and getting away with maybe $18 to $25?"

He wasn't smiling. "Are you sure we understand each other?"

I said, "I hear what you're saying."

"Well, you're not agreeing to it."

I met his gaze straight on and said, "I don't have to agree to it. I was minding my own business in class."

There was a nod of his head and a look settled on his face. "So, you're starting to be defiant already."

I stood my ground. "I'm not starting anything at all. You called me down here from class for absolutely no reason at all. I haven't done anything except attend school."

"Keep talking like that and I'm going to send you home."

I said, "Well, make up your mind. Are you sending me back to class or are you sending me home?"

Another shake of his head. "I don't think we're going to make it."

I wasn't letting it go. "It sounds like you are copying the comments of jails, reform schools, detention homes. This is supposed to be a school and I haven't done one single thing wrong." I said, "So what's your verdict?"

He looked at me and instructed, "Return to class."

The following Tuesday, I met with my parole officer as requested. He started in giving me a lecture. In reaction, I just basically stood up and raked everything off of his desk and looked him in the face. "This is crap. The institution that y'all have created is enough to drive anyone absolutely insane, let alone cause anger and resentment for everything y'all stand for. I haven't done anything wrong and everything seems to be going in a negative direction."

There was a sigh from the officer. "We'll try to work it out." He didn't stand or try to retrieve the items that now laid on the floor, but just said, "Darryl, I'll see you next Tuesday."

He had surprised me. Interacting with him was not what I had expected. He was sensitive, reasonable, and seemingly caring. I certainly wasn't used to this.

It wasn't long before I knew that I needed a car, but I was not going to ask for any help from my grandparents or my mother to get it.

I walked over to Scenic Highway, where several of the local used car lots were, and found one that I liked a lot. I called my father from the sales office. "I'm at a car lot and I need your opinion on one that I've picked out. Can you meet me over here? It's extremely important."

He wasn't used to me asking him for anything, especially not for his opinion. He showed up shortly after I hung up and we spent some time looking over the particular car that I had found. He agreed that it was a good choice. I looked him in the face and said, "Great. Then write the man a check."

There was a quick double-take from my father and the smile quickly left his face. "What do you mean?" he said.

"Write the man a check to pay for the car," I said.

He was incredulous. "I damn sure didn't come over here to buy you a car."

"I'm aware of that, but that's what you're going to do. Otherwise, I'm going to the district attorney in the morning to tell him how many years you haven't paid the child support owed for me and my sister." He studied me for a moment. "If you think it's a joke, try me. They'll have you arrested and you'll have to pay for all the years you never paid a single dime."

I knew that none of the monthly payments had come to my mom for the last ten years of my life, much less any support for my sister. He knew that I knew the prosecutor personally since he lived across the street from my grandmother. He wrote out the check and I was able to drive off the lot with my first car.

It was bound to happen sooner or later. A round of words between me and another student resulted in my being asked if I wanted to settle our issues after school. We were to meet at the Catholic high school across the street from our own Baton Rouge High School that same afternoon.

He was about six feet tall and weighed in at about 180 pounds. His hobby was weightlifting. The rest of the day stories kept getting back to me about his bragging that he was going to "whip my ass beyond belief."

About 200 kids were in attendance to witness our fight, which wound up being very one-sided. He never landed one punch and I got in about 25 licks on him. And my own group stopped it because I was getting madder and madder and hitting him harder and harder.

Several squad cars pulled up. A third of the people ran, the rest backed up and left me and him standing there. The officers asked him, "Did Wheat hit you?"

The boy admitted, "I started it."

One cop said, "I didn't ask you that.

Did Wheat hit you?"

"A lot and I never got to hit him."

One of the officers came over and put handcuffs on me. I was taken to the detention home where I went out back to smoke a cigarette, jumped the fence and wound up walking and hitching a ride to Nanny's house. Nanny heard the full story and called the parole officer. I heard her telling him what happened, that I didn't start the fight and that the other boy had admitted to starting

> *"Life is full of obstacles. I showed you the glass is half full and half empty. It's your choice. Any obstacle can bring you down. Or you can decide that none of them will ever bring you down."*
>
> **Nanny**

the fight without the police doing anything to him, that I had been the only one held responsible.

Squad cars pulled up and the parole officer, after talking to Nanny, persuaded them that he had control of the situation. After they left, he turned around to me. "Would you please try to settle down?"

In sincerity, I told him, "I'll try."

In October, I made the decision to give up on classes and do my own reading like I'd done in the ninth grade. I didn't like the structure of school. I didn't like the tests. And a lot of times what the teachers centered their attention on I found meaningless and useless. So, I went back to my books and brought them to school every day to read. This time, I started on Somerset Maugham, Tennessee Williams, Hemingway, "The Mansion" by Faulkner, one of Dostoyevsky's books, Thomas Wolfe, and John Steinbeck. I would read a lot of books by one of the authors, then move to the next author and read a lot of books by that author. The teachers and I both got used to it…or they tolerated it.

The evenings and weekends were full of distractions. Now that I had a car, I went to dances, bars, and night clubs that were out of town. Some were very rough, like in New Rhodes, Port Allen, Houma, and other places across the river in Baton Rouge and in New Orleans. I spent a great deal of time circling and meeting people at Hopper's Drive-In on Florida Street in Baton Rouge.

You would always see people that you knew. There were a lot of girls in these places too and I got along with them pretty well, making friends with a lot of them.

When the end of school rolled around in May, I was notified that I had failed the tenth grade. I had been labeled a tenth grader in L.T.I., so I guess I had failed twice.

The hot summer months were spent getting back in the habit of stealing and writing hot checks. I did attempt to work several jobs, though. I started out bagging at A&P Grocery Store on Acadian Throughway but ended up getting myself fired. After that, I went to work at a local grocery store but bad things happened. The owner screamed, hollered, and criticized a mentally-handicapped young man who made deliveries for him on a bicycle. One day I had had enough of him abusing the deliverer and let him know my opinion. The owner put his hands on his hips and asked me what was I going to do about it. After I knocked him down three times, he ran down the street to another business and had me picked up and charged with assault and battery. Initially, there was going to be a hearing but nothing ever came of it.

Whatever money I could make that summer, whether legally or illegally, was spent on gas, riding around, or books that I wanted to read.

September rolled around and I was back in school, and back in the tenth grade for the third time. Algebra was one of my classes. Since it was complex, I took the book home and spent the whole weekend reading and learning algebra and completing all the exercises. I hardly slept all weekend and worked at Nanny's kitchen table. I completed all of the tests at the end of each of the chapters—for the whole book. On Tuesday, I walked into the classroom and set the whole year's worth of work on the teacher's desk. My algebra teacher started thumbing through the work, finally realizing what it represented. She looked at me and said, in front of the classroom, "You're a liar. No one can do this amount of work in a couple of days."

I stood up and said, "What's the matter with you? Are you crazy? You don't call students a liar when I have proof that I did this legitimately unless you're calling my grandmother and grandfather liars."

One of my classmates had been in L.T.I. with me and he stood up and told her from where he was standing, "Darryl doesn't lie. He's telling you the truth. Quit picking on him. If he said he did it, he did it."

She left the classroom to go downstairs to "report me." In a few minutes, someone came to escort me downstairs to the principal's office. The principal promptly informed me upon my arrival that I was due for a paddling for my lying.

"I didn't lie. You can ask my grandparents. I did the whole algebra book plus the tests at the end of each chapter."

"The teacher called you a liar because no one is capable of doing that.

You've only been in school a couple of weeks."

I tried to explain. I said, "At first, I didn't think I could do it either. Then I started to catch on and I stayed up almost all night and all day until I finished the whole book."

The principal said, "I don't believe you and I'm going to paddle you."

I reached over and shut the door and locked it. "If you really want to do this, then we can really do it. If you hit me with that board, then I promise you it will end up in your throat. You have my word that only one of us will walk out of this office alive if you hit me with that board."

The principal yelled through the locked door for his secretary to call the police. When they arrived, Nanny was with them as well. She walked in and proceeded to berate the principal for how I had been mistreated and targeted since my coming back to school from L.T.I. When the discussion went to the subject of paddling, she offered a choice, that instead of paddling I could be expelled for a week and then come back.

The principal actually said, "No. Because I want to give him a paddling. I'm the principal of this school."

I jumped in with Nanny and the police standing there. "Again, if you hit me with that board you will regret it. I'll get the board and beat you half to death with it. If you want to fight, say so."

"Then in that case," he said to his secretary, "Darryl Wheat is permanently expelled from Baton Rouge High School."

With those words, two things happened...I walked out of the school with the head of juvenile court and my parole officer with my high school days finished. And, secondly, I was not going to graduate from Baton Rouge High School.

Apparently, the principal reported my threat and a court hearing was set for several days later. My parole officer pleaded my case, telling the judge that I had a job and was working and that basically, I hadn't done anything wrong.

I turned to look at this man who was saying both valid and compassionate things about me and my situation. I said, "Why are you doing this?"

He smiled at me and said, "Just because."

But I wheeled around and spoke my next words to the man sitting in front of me in the black robe. "The world that you've picked out here, I don't really fit in anymore, Your Honor. I don't fit in because you sent me to a place that you know is horrible and how they really treat children. When is the last time you've gone down there yourself? No. You just sit on the judge's stand and say words. You have no experience with that place. Or, if you do, then you're out of your mind."

The judge interrupted me. "Darryl Wheat, if you don't shut up I'm going to put you in jail."

Undeterred by this, I continued. "You do what you want to do. What you're doing this morning is trying to get out from under the accusation and knowledge that you're sending children to a place where they're treated cruelly, taught to be criminals, where there's nobody to help them, nobody to talk to them, nobody who cares about them in the facility, and where, behind closed doors, they do all sorts of bizarre things to the children there."

The judge exploded with, "That does it. I'm giving you 15 days on the pea farm."

"Your Honor, you're just a little bit late. They put me on a pea farm in L.T.I. on a Saturday when it was raining. Go down there some time so you can see the consequences of your action."

"I'm going to give you 15 more days if you don't shut up."

I looked over my shoulder as they were escorting me from the courtroom and said, "Do whatever you have to do."

I was taken to the East Baton Rouge Parish Jail to start serving my 15 days. I was booked and put in a day room cell with about ten other people charged with DUIs, domestic violence, and one even serving several years there at the parish prison. We were to weed and take care of the peas at the pea farm. It was hot as blue blazes, and, if it drizzled rain, we were to continue working. That night as I was sitting and smoking cigarettes I thought up an interesting plan.

I told the other inmates about how we could do something interesting. In the early part of the evening on a night that it rained, we could dig a large hole behind the barn. If we pulled up all the pea plants, the ones that had been farmed at that location for 20 years, and buried them in the hole, covering them back over with mud, we would never be caught. In preparation, I turned one of the window screens around so that the screws were on the inside, which would allow us to get out without anyone knowing. The first night it rained, we took off all our clothes, leaving them inside where they remained dry and clean while we became very muddy carrying out our plan. It was a long night but 15 to 20 rows of peas that ran about 50 yards in length disappeared completely. When we had finished, we came back in through the window, showered and put back on our dry, clean clothes. There was no evidence left anywhere of us having done anything that night.

The next morning, we were called out and told to line up outside the house. The assistants for the farm as well as the deputies in charge of us were in attendance. The owner came out and asked why no one was working. Everyone pointed to the field. There were no peas. He turned around to look at the field and then went to pieces. He got hysterical and wanted to know where his peas were. "For years, I've been raising peas. Where are my peas?"

The deputies were having problems trying not to laugh, especially when the owner went to each one asking about his peas and no one could answer. He asked each of the inmates and no one was saying a word. "Where are my peas?" Turning to the deputies again, he demanded, "One of these men knows where these peas are. Have you interviewed them? Make them tell you where the peas are."

An officer said, "I did. Wheat is the only one who offered an explanation."

"Then what?"

"Wheat said maybe a flying saucer came by and they were hungry." The owner came over and grabbed me. "Are you some kind of a nut?" I said, "No, sir. But I do have something to ask you."

"What? What?"

I said, "Where are your peas?"

He started stomping around again.

To my knowledge, that was the last time East Baton Rouge Parish Jail ever ran a pea farm. I have to say I loved the plan.

I was transferred to the detention home and back up to the jail to finish out my 15 days. I left a note with the judge's secretary upstairs on the second floor of the courthouse saying this, "Where are this man's peas?"

At the age of 16, my arrest record was becoming very extensive, filled with a large number of arrests, numerous sentences, misdemeanors, felonies, a stint in reform school, detention homes, jails, being expelled from school, and apparently an inability to find the right job.

My father introduced me to the local welders and pipefitters union. I learned different tasks from working in fabrication shops and short-term work on pipelines. I had a card as a welder helper or a pipefitter helper. I liked the jobs. They were dangerous and hard, but I developed a reputation that helped me become a helper on almost any job that they had. I was so used to working in L.T.I. that working hard in the steel and fabrication shops came easy to me. And I loved working on the pipelines.

But at the end of the day, no matter what had happened during the day, I could always count on going home to Nanny. She was my one constant. Nanny was always my supporter—breakfast and coffee with Nanny in the morning, her handing me a bag with a sandwich in it for lunch, and asking me all about it when I came home. She always knew what I was thinking and feeling. She knew me like the palm of her hand.

Most of all, she believed in me.

Age: 16
Location: Baton Rouge,
Louisiana

# You have to help a friend, but...

Being kicked out of school permanently, I was now working pipelines on a full-time basis. During the week, every morning I spent having breakfast and coffee with Nanny. Even at night after returning, if I was able to return, she taught. I listened. My problem was—A lack of application of what I had learned from Nanny.

In spite of what I had already been through, my weekends were given to drinking, parties, dances, and wildness. One specific place that all Baton Rougeans went was to Hoppers Drive-in on Florida Street, just meeting people, drinking a shake, saying hello, or getting into a fight. It seems like I had at least one fight every weekend. If so, then I would be the one taken down to the station, blamed for the incident, jailed, and charged with assault and battery or simple assault. Sometimes I would be transferred to the detention home and sometimes my parole officer would come to get me and take me back to Nanny's house. The reason I even mention that is to underline the fact that once you get a bad reputation with the police and correctional officers you can't get rid of it. You're forever blamed for things you did and didn't do.

In the midst of this "busy" schedule, one of my friends who had been incarcerated later than all of us, contacted me asking for help. It seemed that he had "released" himself (escaped) from L.T.I., stolen a car, and was back in the area. Together, we forged some checks for spending money, switched out the license plate on the car and made some other modifications to disguise it. We got him some clothes and went around seeing some of our friends. At the end of the night, the car was parked in a place where he could sleep in it without being noticed and plans were made for the next day.

Within an hour of showing up at a friend's house the next morning, we were surrounded by the police and taken to the station, charged and booked. He was charged with car theft and correctional escape. I was charged with car theft, aiding an escapee, and suspicion of forgery. I don't know where they put him but they put me in solitary confinement.

It's very difficult to tell time in solitary confinement. The only light in the room is in the ceiling, about ten feet off the floor, and it never goes off. I was allowed a jail t-shirt and some long pants. The size of the solitary confinement cell was about the size of a hall closet, so there wasn't much room to move around. Bathroom facilities consisted of a hole in the middle of the floor. Food was served on a tray that was slid through an opening at the bottom of the door and was allowed to bounce and spill if you didn't get it in time. In other words, cold coffee could be all over a small number of eggs, a spoonful of grits and a piece of bread.

I tried to catch my tray in the mornings and evenings. I would usually say things like, "Hey, the coffee is fantastic but, if you would be so kind, would you include

*When you're in solitary confinement, you have to work on your sanity. You're in a small room with no one to talk to, no way to tell time, no way to tell whether it's day or night. And, unless you have some defense against the drastic-ness of this confinement, you could come apart pretty easily. Your tendency in solitary is to want to fight it. The tendency to visualize or think about negative things becomes natural unless you use a survival method.*

*I had learned from Nanny that when your mind centers on negative thoughts that you could neutralize them with "affirmations." She had started teaching me about affirmations from the time when I was about five years old. What I learned is when you use affirmations over and over for a long period of time they become part of you and your beliefs. So, every time I was in solitary confinement I always turned to that method of mental survival.*

a little more sweetener?" Of course, this incensed the guards dramatically but most of them at the Baton Rouge jail knew me already.

I could only guess that some days passed and I was escorted downstairs to a room where my friend and three detectives were waiting. He was quick on the trigger. Before they could stop him, he looked at me and said, "The car was stolen."

I caught the gift he had just thrown to me. I put a surprised expression on my face and stated, "Why didn't you tell me?"

He said, "Because you probably wouldn't have helped me if you had known it was a stolen car."

This short exchange between us was meant to fool the detectives and to do what he could to keep me being sent back to L.T.I. with him. If I was found to have any part of the stolen car, I certainly would be going back there shortly.

I was then ushered into another office to see my parole officer. He looked a little sad, but he just said, "Are you okay?"

I just said, "Yeah."

"Then I'm going to get you out of here and take you home. I've put in a request to meet with the judge about your parole violation. You're being charged with aiding a runaway, a stolen car, suspicion of forgery. I'll do most of the talking and, on this rare occasion, you will shut up. You'll open your mouth and get yourself sent back." He said, "This is a close call but I think we'll win this."

He gave me a ride home to Nanny. Out of hell with a 24-hour light in the ceiling to a heaven called 2755 Washington Avenue to have coffee with someone that has a personal conversation with God every day.

Age: 17
Location: Baton Rouge,
Louisiana

# 16

# The great train robbery (Not!)....

My group was out cruising one night (obviously we didn't have enough to do!) when one of the members remembered a train on the tracks by the Louisiana State University campus. What had caught his attention was the boxcar with Budweiser boldly painted on the side of it, and we were determined that free beer was going to be had that night. Once there, we easily opened the door of the boxcar and were loading what we could grab into the trunk of our car when it became obvious the bottles were not heavy enough – that we had gotten into a load of empties headed back to the company to be recycled. In the midst of this discovery, suddenly police car sirens could be heard coming from just about every direction. We didn't know that we had been spotted by a night watchman at the train yard who had alerted the police.

We all loaded into the car, the best driver in town behind the wheel, and took off trying to shake them— through neighborhoods, under bridges, through creeks.

After an hour, it became obvious they were catching up to us and we would eventually be caught. The car was stopped behind LSU stadium and we all piled out and lit up cigarettes while waiting for the six or seven police cars that came skidding in from every direction—the middle of LSU, Nicholson Drive, Perkins Road.

They took all of us down to the station where we were questioned. All of us had either been in L.T.I. or jail and ranged in age of 16 to 17. We knew how to handle the questioning process because we knew the street code of refusing to say anything about the crime or anyone's involvement in it. You didn't "rat" and we all lived by that code.

Even though we didn't talk during the questioning, we were told about our charges—that we not only had robbed the train but had also broken a federal seal when we opened the boxcar. That meant that we had committed a federal offense as well as stealing empty beer bottles.

We were all booked but I was the only one put into solitary confinement. I asked why and I was told that my record of escapes and runaways dictated it.

After a couple of days, we were all brought together into a room with an FBI agent who had come in from Atlanta, Georgia. He was very relaxed, professional and calm in his seersucker suit with the exception of using his hat to fan himself. His first question—"Is Baton Rouge always this humid?" It was obvious he had acquainted himself with our actions two days before and with us as individuals. He explained the federal offense that we had committed and then started singling each one of us out regarding the consequences of our actions. I had the honor of being first. "Darryl, you're 17 now and you'll be tried as an adult and you'll be going to Leavenworth. Because of your runaways and escapes, parole will not be an option for you. You'll probably get five years and serve every day of it." He went around the room and told the rest of the group the length of each one's sentence and how long they would probably serve.

But, in speaking to the group, he said, "There's another alternative. I'm going to give you an option to consider. If you say that you broke into the warehouse and went to the side of the train, and didn't break the seal on the boxcar, then I'll drop federal charges and you'll be turned over to the State of Louisiana." He knew we had broken the seal. He explained that the situation really wasn't worth it for the feds to take us to Atlanta and charge us for breaking into a boxcar and stealing empty beer bottles. But he confirmed this, "I assure you that each of you is going to make up your mind and tell me that story or you're all going back with me on the plane to Atlanta to be charged with a federal offense and sent to respective penitentiaries."

I hadn't been able to talk to any of the group, but I had not expected an alternative to be offered. The next surprise was him telling the police officer in the room to take our handcuffs off and to get each of us Coca Colas, hamburgers, and a pack of cigarettes. When the officer questioned him, the agent told him, "I'm running this. Do what I told you to do." He seemed calm as a cucumber and in total control. "I'm not worried about y'all running away. This is not a state offense. It's a federal offense. You wouldn't make it ten miles outside of Baton Rouge or go near any boat, ship or plane before you'd be stopped by the Federal Bureau of Investigation."

He continued. "I will see you in two days, on Monday morning at 10:00 with your admission that you went through an open warehouse into an open boxcar. Then I will leave and go back to Atlanta and y'all will stay here. Have a good weekend."

We looked at each other after the agent left the room and the police told us we could leave with our food and cigarettes. We all knew the street code we lived by—you don't "rat" on yourself or anybody else and you don't admit to any crime whatsoever. We all agreed to meet Sunday at Sacred Heart Church and to figure out what to do. I was unable to be of any help because I found it impossible to confess to a crime that I knew I would serve five years for. There were six of us.

Monday morning, we met at the newsstand across the street from the police station and walked in together. We were led to the same room where the meeting with the agent had been held on Saturday. He started off with the weather again. "It's even hot when you go for a walk after dark in Baton Rouge. But I can say this, there is no food as tasty as Cajun cooking. I had a great supper. Incidentally, y'all can all relax. An admission has

> *"You can change and control what you think, gain self-mastery, direct your own destiny, and start a new journey toward the life you have always wanted."*
> **Nanny**

been made that all of you went through an open door in the warehouse and stepped from the warehouse into an open boxcar. There was no federal seal to your knowledge and y'all didn't break it."

We looked at each other around the table. Somebody had met with him and confessed.

He continued to speak about what would happen in the future. I would be charged with burglary (the warehouse), but no federal charges would be filed and I would be turned over to the State of Louisiana. A date had been set for my court hearing but I would be released until then. "Ha. You can thank me for that.

The local police would rather have contained you," the agent said with a wink in my direction.

A week later, my parole officer visited me and told me that there were no federal charges and that the State of Louisiana was not going to spend its time charging me for walking through a warehouse for a burglary, which typically carried a nine-year sentence. The rest of the news he shared was slightly less bizarre. I was getting credit for time served. *Can you even believe that? Two days in jail and credit for time served for burglarizing a warehouse. Okay. Whatever!*

So at 17, I wasn't going to the state penitentiary and I wasn't going back to L.T.I. I was going back to Nanny's house and going back to work on pipelines. Things could have turned out very differently!

# 17

# Trouble followed
# me east...

My activities continued to be wild with arrests and questioning happening frequently. It was no longer something that happened, but rather a way of life.

I had become acquainted with a cook in a restaurant on Third Street who was telling me about an upcoming trip he and his girlfriend were planning. Their first stop was to be in Georgia where he would introduce his family to the girl he would be marrying in Alabama on their way back to Baton Rouge. I was invited to go along on the trip and the thought of getting out of town was appealing, but there was another motive for taking him up on the invitation. The girl I had been dating recently moved to Texas and, if she could be included, the four of us could make the trip together. He had no problems with changing the route and we backtracked to Texas before we started heading east.

Not long after the four of us had gotten settled into the car, the cook revealed that the car we were in was one he had test-driven off a lot and never returned. We were driving halfway across the country in a stolen car! I knew nothing about this part of the plans!

Here we go again! A stolen car and crossing a bunch of state lines, each of which carries its own laws and penalties!

There were no problems on our way to Georgia and the visit with his mother went well. After a couple of days, we were back on the road again, traveling through the Florida panhandle to get to a small Alabama town where the wedding was to take place.

My girlfriend and I, after some discussion, announced that we would be joining our companions in a double ceremony when we arrived. I was 17 and she was 15, but the law for that state only required males to be a minimum of 16 and females 14 to be legally married. We met the requirements and the vows were exchanged.

The first stop after leaving the courthouse was the local Western Union office. We were all broke and I called my uncle asking him to wire me some money so we could make it back to Baton Rouge. Not long after I hung up from my phone call with him, we were surrounded by police cars and taken to the county jail. He had called either my grandmother or my mother who in turn had called the police.

During the next three days, my companion and his now-wife had several conversations with the police and the car dealership in Baton Rouge. Arrangements were made to buy the car as soon as they returned and they were released from the Alabama jail. The following day, the girl I had married was picked up by her parents and taken back to Texas.

I was left to face the consequences of my part in all of this. During the months that followed, I was interrogated numerous times, beaten often, placed in solitary confinement regularly, and told that I had a "cocky mouth." I made sure to inform them that I had no respect for the way they treated inmates.

Eventually, I was able to obtain a stamp and envelope to send Nanny a letter. I told her where I was and the different charges that were being brought against me by the states through which we had traveled. Texas was trying to extradite me from Alabama and their charges included contributing to the delinquency of a juvenile and kidnapping (which by itself carried a 20-year sentence). Georgia wanted to charge me with auto theft. Alabama had charged me and booked me for kidnapping, auto theft, and contributing to the delinquency of a juvenile. And, if I managed to get back to Louisiana, they were going to charge me with auto theft and parole violations.

It turns out that each state takes its turn sentencing you on the charges they bring and you serve time for those charges.

> 'Just remember to have bulldog' tenacity. Never let them break you. And don't forget that life is actually wonderful.
> **Nanny**

The next state meets you at the gate, transfers you, sentences you and you serve time for their charges. In other words, the charges I was now facing from all states involved would encompass about 25 years of my life.

Nanny answered my letter with words of encouragement. Her response was "pure Nanny." She explained that when Texas extradited me, an attorney would be hired and they would come there, but coming to Alabama seemed to be futile and useless at that current time.

So, there I sat in a small Alabama jail for months until I faced a kangaroo court at 5:30 in the morning and was released, told to get out of the state of Alabama. I set my sights on getting back home…to Nanny.

# 18

# I just wanted to get home, but...

Thumbing a ride out of Alabama got me as far as Gulfport, Mississippi where I spent the night under a pier on the beach. Traffic woke me the next morning and I was cold and hungry. Across the street was a restaurant called the Friendship House and I went around to the back door in hopes of bumming some breakfast from the cook, but I was stopped on the way by a police car pulling up behind me. One of the officers came over and questioned what I was doing, accused me of loitering, and told me to pour the contents of the bag I was carrying onto the ground. I complied and, finding nothing of interest, he told me to pick everything back up. I did as I was told.

It was obvious that the plans I had for breakfast were not going to work out. Attempting to cross back to the other side of the street, I walked past the second officer, who had observed my previous conversation and actions with his partner. He grabbed the bag out of my hands and dumped everything on the ground again. After his search through my belongings, and him not finding anything either, I was again told to pick everything up.

"No, I'm not picking them up anymore." I was told, "Pick them up or go to jail."

"You poured them out. I don't want them anymore and I'm not going to pick them up." I was arrested on the spot.

They took me to a jail that, I guess, was in Gulfport. In the booking area, the small ink pad used for fingerprinting was too dry to put a good image on the paper, so they were not able to identify me through that process. And I certainly didn't volunteer any information about who I was or where I lived. They wound up placing me in a holding cell with about nine or ten other prisoners overnight.

The new sponge had not yet made it to the jail the following morning by the time a large truck came and everyone was loaded to go out and work on a work gang that cut grass on the side of the road. I was herded into the truck along with all the other prisoners without any questions or comments.

Around mid-morning, a blacktop rolling machine, working adjacent to us and blacktopping a narrow street, frustrated a driver that needed to get around it. The guards were on the backside of the machine and I was out of their sight. I ran over and knocked on the window, getting the attention of an older couple. The female in the driver's seat rolled down the window and

I talked quickly. I told them these were fearful people, that they were convicts and that I didn't want to walk down the street near them. I asked if there was any way they could give me a ride to the Friendship House. They said, "Sure. Get in." They made their way around the slow machine and we were able to leave the area.

The police still didn't know who I was or have my fingerprints but those guards would know that I wasn't on the work crew in just a few minutes. I knew the only two people who could identify me were the two policemen and the guy who tried to fingerprint me and so I needed to avoid them until I could leave town. Further down the street, there was a "For Rent" sign in front of a house that I managed to use for cover until it got dark.

Once it was nightfall, I started down the road in the direction of Long Beach, Mississippi, until a driver picked me up and took me to Covington, Louisiana. From there, I was able to get another ride all the way back to home

*Goodness gracious, I had actually arrived back in Baton Rouge!*

I was able to make it to 2755 Washington Avenue, to Nanny and my grandfather; to pass the two chinaberry trees in the front yard, to see the

> *"Success and accomplishment are based on your thoughts, your beliefs, your commitment, your determination, and your perseverance."*
>
> **Nanny**

ten crepe myrtle trees on the side street, and to sit on the back porch privately hidden by ten-foot-tall Ligustrum. Almost all of Nanny's teachings had occurred on that back porch. It was like a holy spot that was always in my thoughts and dreams, like a safety curtain from the world. I slept very well that night for the first time in a long time.

The following morning, we had coffee and breakfast together. There were some tough stories to tell her about all that I had been through, including the fact that I had gotten married. As it turned out, divorce would follow shortly down the road but I didn't know that then. She listened carefully and took it seriously as I told her about the kangaroo court, coming back through Mississippi, being arrested and how I got away.

The following morning we followed our usual routine of coffee and breakfast, and our conversation continued. She had been thinking about the things that I had said the day before and she had a question. She wanted to know if I thought there was some universal project being enforced to keep me alive and keep me well for some purpose. I smiled and asked her if that was what she thought. She said, "Makes you wonder about many of the great people in history who started from a minus only to end up on a mountaintop for mankind. Maybe the Creator has something special for you."

Several hours later, the city police picked me up and took me downtown where the head of both the juvenile and detective divisions met with me and my parole officer. I was told that Georgia and Alabama would not respond to any stolen car cases across state lines because the man who had paid for it when he returned to Baton Rouge. All kidnapping charges were no longer valid since we were found to be of legal age by state law in Alabama where the marriage was performed, which also took care of all cases pending of contributing to the delinquency of a juvenile in any of the states including Texas.

However, they did say that I had violated parole in numerous ways and my parole officer and I would attend a court hearing over this. I was informed that I now had accrued over 12 parole violations.

I met with my parole officer on Nanny's front porch the following morning. He said he was going to take care of the hearing and for me not to worry about it. I was not going to be charged or sentenced for any of the parole violations.

Nanny got Mr. Cooper some coffee and they talked. He had a huge respect for her and frequently processed these kinds of experiences or findings with her, but it was his efforts that kept me from further legal matters over this situation and many others.

I spent several days recuperating mentally from everything that had gone on. And each morning included coffee and breakfast with Nanny combined with great conversations.

Age: 18
Location: Baton Rouge,
Louisiana

## 19

# Everyone has limits...

I was pacing up and down in an Alabama jail on my 18<sup>th</sup> birthday but, now that I was back in town, I needed to register for the draft.

*Oh, Lord. Okay. I don't want to be charged for dodging the draft on top of everything else.*

A friend bummed a ride from me the day I went to the recruiting station. We were going to do something together after I was through but he went across the street to the library until I was ready. Inside the door, I was greeted by a recruiter who was about 6'2" and weighed probably about 230 pounds. He was in full-dress uniform and directed me upstairs when I told him what I was trying to do. At the top of the stairs was a woman sitting behind a card table with what looked like notes or a file of some kind and I could see that my name was on some of the paperwork in front of her.

I stood in front of the table ready to act on whatever instructions she was about to give me to complete the process. She asked me to sit down and, while she was thumbing through some papers, I asked if she was the one who figured out the rank I should have. Her response was, "Yes, but before I do that I want to ask you some questions." I figured she would need to know some things about me, but the questions she asked were not what I expected. Nor were they ones I wanted to answer...

One question she asked was why I didn't file a battery charge against my father for hitting my mother when I was four years old. Another question asked was, if my mother loved me so much, why had she left me as well as not come to any of my court hearings.

*How did she get this information on me and access to my file? Was this traditional in signing up for the draft? What in the world was she doing with all of this information and how did she get it? I guess from a federal standpoint she could get anything she wanted to get. How would I know?*

I looked her straight in the face and asked her if we could stop this, that all I had come to do was to sign the paperwork required to register for the draft. That didn't stop her questions from coming. Again, I asked her to stop with the questions. "If you have notes, use them, but I don't want to talk about any of this."

But she kept on and her next question was, "Why didn't your grandmother step in?"

Adrenaline flooded me. I didn't answer her but it was because I couldn't. I just stared at her. I could feel my body reacting as it did right before a fight: loss of breath, overwhelmed, can't talk. *How dare she bring up my grandmother!* I felt myself losing control.

One more question. "Why did you run away from home?"

*That did it!*

I reached under the table and flipped it over sending all of her paperwork flying across the room. "I'm leaving," and started in the direction of the stairs.

Her reaction was to yell to the man downstairs to stop me. That seemed strange because he was only a recruiter as far as I knew and I wondered what right he had in doing anything to me.

By the time I started down the stairs, he had positioned himself at the bottom fully blocking my descent. He was huge. I wasn't hesitant. When I got to the bottom, I hit him in the face with all I had and sent him backward into a bookcase that then fell on top of him as I was walking out of the recruitment office's front door.

> *"Courage is a choice. How you choose to respond is your choice."*
> **Nanny**

My friend was crossing the street in my direction and could tell something was wrong. "Are you okay?"

I said, "No. I just got into a fight." My friend was shaking his head as I was describing what had just happened.

He said, "That doesn't make any sense. All the rest of us just went in and signed the paper. But I don't know what they can do to you."

But we were soon to find out because, before I could get my car started, one car with two people in it pulled up blocking me from leaving. It was a federal car.

At about the same moment, a Baton Rouge police car pulled up and Frank Thomas from the juvenile division got out and approached the officers and me. I don't know how he knew what happened unless he heard it come across the police radio.

One of the MPs started the discussion by saying that the man inside the recruiting station wanted to charge me with assault. Mr. Thomas interrupted him. "We have a problem over jurisdiction and territory. You may argue that the territory inside that building is federal grounds if you wish. I'm not a federal attorney but presently this boy is on the sidewalk in Baton Rouge in the state of Louisiana and you have no jurisdiction whatsoever. Now, if he wants to file in federal court, it's around in front of the library facing Florida Street. If he wants to file citizen charges, he needs to go down to the police station and file there."

The recruiter came out onto the street and yelled, "Let me tell you what happened."

Mr. Thomas was not willing to listen. "We're taking him in the car and I don't care what happened. The officers have been told how and where to file whatever charges you find necessary," and my friend and I were quickly pushed toward the Baton Rouge police car.

After the car doors shut, Mr. Thomas swiveled around from the driver's seat to look at me. "Why don't you just go out to the zoo and fight a gorilla?" Obviously, he had noticed the size of the man I had chosen to hit.

Two or three weeks later, I received a form letter informing me that aggravated battery charges had been filed in the downtown police department but had been dropped due to the recruiter's inability to explain why he had the right to hold me physically and confine me in the building.

Also, included was my draft card ranking me as 4-F. That was as upsetting to me as anything that had happened. I had no desire to be drafted, but I also didn't think I deserved 4-F. I asked around my group and not one single one of them had received that kind of a rating. The whole thing to me was crazy. Other than a few relevant questions, I'm positive nothing the woman had asked should have been used to determine my fitness for military duty.

Age: 18
Location: Baton Rouge,
Louisiana

$\boxed{20}$

# The man in the mirror...

So much had happened in my 18 years of life and I was starting to do some serious introspection. I continued to enjoy my time every morning with Nanny over coffee and breakfast. Our conversations were always deep with her asking questions, and the topics of our discussions were soul searching. The words of wisdom she shared gave me something to look forward to every day.

I was back to pipeline work but, every available minute of the day, even while I was driving (which made people nervous!), was spent burying myself in a book. The books I read were about great people, brave people, famous people, especially the individuals who had worked their way up in life from what seemed to be zero to find their mountaintop. Nanny was offering books and book titles in a way to guide me on how to climb my own mountain. During our time together in the mornings, we would talk about the books and particularly the underlines and notes I had made while reading them. She was great at explaining or helping me to come to my own conclusions about what I could learn from each book I experienced. Every day she worked to fill my head with knowledge and possibilities.

Actually, Nanny had been guiding me on how to get to my own mountaintop since I was five, but at 18 I was realizing that I was actually in a ditch and the mountain that I had created was made of mistakes. My mistakes. I had veered away from everything that Nanny had tried to teach me and everything that I had read about what others had done with their lives. I was also bothered by the 4-F classification that I had received.

I was old enough to know that I had to look at myself and realize there were some serious personal problems. Problems with being excessively sensitive. Problems controlling my anger. Problems with being on the verge of fighting all the time and being sarcastic to authority figures. I had family and friends available to me, yet I felt so personally alone. These realizations about who I was were weighing heavily on me.

I started counting off some of my self-discoveries: I was lacking a direction. I had made a life of being self-destructive. I had no conscience about committing crimes anymore. I had learned to be clever, devious, dishonest, and other strategies that had allowed me to survive on the streets.

I realized the stress I had put myself under out on the streets, serving time in jail, being put in reform schools, useless correctional escapes. But I had experienced other things that were having an impact on who I was—police beatings, guards burning me with their cigarettes, the risk to my sanity from spending time in solitary confinement. All of these had caused so much trauma that I was no longer myself. Nor did I even know who I should be.

At 13, playing Little League baseball, I had won 11 games and pitched eight no-hitters. At 18, I was now an accomplished criminal able to steal from any store, to forge checks, to sit and figure out how to burglarize almost any place. But my time in the Alabama jail had put me dangerously close to serving a long prison sentence and had started my adult criminal file. Everything up to then had been a part of my juvenile record but at 18 I had started writing a new chapter in my rap sheet.

I had learned to hurt people when I fought. As I was getting older, I was being held in more dangerous jails with more aggressive criminals, which meant that my opponents were getting bigger and more serious about hurting me and I had to be more serious about protecting myself from being hurt. The fighting now had serious consequences— physically and, as it turned out, mentally.

There was no particular purpose that I was committed to, no achievement or dream, nothing great that I was trying to

> *"Great achievers, after much hard work and attitude change, refuse to be defeated by setbacks, disappointments, or problems that are usually defined as 'failures.'"*
>
> **Nanny**

do with my life. I was just spending time reading about others, but I had not applied anything that I had learned to my own daily living. Instead, I was relying on street smarts to exist in jails, reform school, and to cope with authority figures. While I had lost the fear of dangerous situations and dangerous people, I had also lost the ingredients that go with good judgment.

All the members of the group that I ran with had found jobs that would help them fit into society and make a living. My temper had gotten in my way and kept me from being able to hold a job for any length of time so far.

I determined that my current job of being a welder's helper needed to work out.

Nanny's comment of, "Maybe the universe is trying to tell you something," had been made before I started the pipeline work and some of the recent happenings on the job made me think about that statement. One of my first jobs was to help a welder who had climbed a 50 to 60 foot scaffold and I was to follow. The scaffold came to pieces before I was on it and the welder fell and died on the way to the hospital. One of the next jobs was with a welder who drowned when his truck turned over as he was going through a Louisiana swamp. Another job had me in town getting lunch for the crew I was working with. While I was gone, one person slipped and grabbed two others causing them all to fall in front of the 90-inch pipeline that was full of gas which the welding equipment caused to explode and burn. When I returned, the bodies were stretched out in the field covered with white sheets. Mine could easily have been added to make the count one more if I had been there. And the fourth incident that got my attention was when a former welder, who was then an administrator, asked me to help him pass his welding test for the pipelines. The morning I was to leave to meet him for the testing, I instead received a call from his family that there had been gas in the pipe he was to be tested on and he had burned to death.

So, my Nanny, my beloved grandmother, my teacher, a true genius in every sense of the term—was she right? Was the universe trying to tell me something? Was I being prepared for a greater team like Nanny had been trying to tell me since I was five years old?

I took a few days to think about these and other thoughts running through my mind, to try to make sense of who I was and where I might be going. Because I couldn't stay where I was.

Age: 18
Location: Baton Rouge,
Louisiana

# 21

# The final straw
# (or pipeline)...

Blackie, the welder that I normally helped, called me at Nanny's and told me about a rush job that was scheduled. The goal was to complete a pipeline placement under a bridge in time for people to be able to use the roadway to return home after work that same afternoon. Not much time to do it but, to make matters worse, the forecast was predicting heavy rain for the next three days.

When I mentioned my concerns about the weather, Blackie brought up some of our past experiences. "We worked through a 35 mile-an-hour wind and snow in Oklahoma. We crossed a swamp on the other side of Lafayette. We welded in a 50-mile-an-hour wind six feet off the ground as well as an oil rig out in the Gulf with water coming across the top. Are you going to be there or not?"

"Of course," was the only answer I could give.

When I got to the site, our equipment was a huge old truck with one welding machine on the back and it was storming with heavy, steady rain. The pipe we were to work on was in a ditch about two-and-a-half feet deep that was already filled with water. This was going to be a nightmare.

The foreman was instructed that we needed some boxes of dry welding rods and some two-by-fours to build a platform so we could be out of the water while we welded. The welding rods were fine but the wood brought in was not solid enough to bear our weight and kept breaking. Blackie and I finally decided that going down into the water was the only way we could get this job done, and our workday was passing quickly with the knowledge the bridge had to be open for the hundreds of cars lined up to use it in a few hours. The truck with the welding machine was up on the bank. With the weather conditions as they were, the power needed to be turned to its highest, which meant that Blackie and I were constantly being shocked as we tried to weld standing in the water. But the foreman was more worried about the gas required to operate the machine at its fullest power and kept instructing his son to turn down the power. When the machine was turned lower, there were times we couldn't strike an arc and, when the welding rods got wet, they were no longer usable and we were throwing out large numbers of them. Nothing was working correctly for us to get this job done.

I climbed the approximately 25-foot muddy embankment on three separate occasions to turn up the machine because Blackie kept throwing back his helmet and saying, "I can't weld. Wheat, I can't weld like this. I don't have enough spark, enough electricity." But every time I turned it up and worked my way back down to where Blackie needed me, the foreman's son went to the truck and turned the power back down.

Blackie was worried. "What's the traffic like?" No plans had been made to reroute the traffic, and at this rate, we were going to be working on into the night before we could re-open the bridge. We weren't physically prepared to change clothes. We were drenched. The storm was picking up and so was the wind.

Blackie threw his welding helmet back and asked, "Do you have any suggestions?"

I said, "Yep." I climbed up the embankment one final time. I started the engine of the truck, backed it up and then hit the accelerator to land the truck, with the welding machine, in the eight-foot-deep water about 20 feet away from where we had been working. When it came to rest, the truck was nose down at the bottom of the 25-foot embankment.

About 25 to 30 construction people, from electricians to bridge builders, stood with their mouths open.

*"There is no power greater than what's already within you. Don't forget to use it."*

**Nanny**

Blackie climbed out of the hole and stood looking at me, almost with a smile.

I started walking down the road towards Baton Rouge and I could hear Blackie and the foreman yelling at each other. The foreman yelled, "You'd better return."

I heard Blackie answer, "In your dreams."

"That boy just ruined a $40,000 truck and a $20,000 welding machine!"

Blackie yelled back, "I'd offer him more money and thank God he didn't beat your son's brains out." Before I had gotten too far down the road, Blackie's truck pulled up alongside me and I got in. We could see in the rear -view mirror that a side-boom was pulling the truck out of the water behind us.

Blackie said, "He'll double your salary. I'll get him to triple your salary if you will come back."

I said, "Blackie, you and I know that they should have built a temporary bridge to give us time to do this. This can't be done, even if we work all night. Also, if we go back, I'm going to make sure his son's not eligible to go to college."

"You don't want to go back?"

There was no hesitation. "I'm not going back. Will you take me back to my car at Delmont Village?

He said, "If you don't go back, I'm not going back." "Take me to my car then."

Blackie said, "Only if I can treat you to Piccadilly when we get back."

"You've got a deal."

We used the restroom at the Texaco Station to change into dry clothes both of us had tucked into our vehicles and got back into his truck to head to the cafeteria. It was a short trip but Blackie commented, "This is the first time I've heard you be this quiet."

"Blackie, you're like a second father to me. I love Baton Rouge with all my might—every street, every alley. I know this town like the palm of my hand, blindfolded. I grew up here. But I can't go on this way. I can't take any more. I feel like just getting into the car and driving in some direction until I run out of gas. Find a place that reads, find a place that learns, find a place that teaches me more, find a place where no one knows who I am. Kind of like college."

He slowed down the truck. "Look at me. You've been working with me off and on since you were 15 or 16. At least 25 percent of that time has been arrests, serving time, probation, parole, fist fighting…"

He continued, "If you went to college, I'd be one of the happiest men on earth. If I have been hard on you, teased you, pushed you, and you end up in a college, it would have been worth it." He added, "You're one of the smartest people I've ever met. I think people resent you for that. You're certainly the most courageous kid that I've ever been around in my life. And your willingness to confront fear ought to be written in a book. I've loved you and admired you. I wish I had had a son like you."

We didn't talk again until we got into the cafeteria when he said, "I want to have coffee with you in the morning at your grandmother's house. Am I invited?"

I said, "Of course."

He said, "I'll see you in the morning."

I said, "I'm counting on it."

Blackie came over to the house the following morning, hugged Nanny, and I gave them time to talk. I got my cup of coffee and went out on the back porch to join them.

He said, "You're not coming back to pipelines, are you?"

I said, "No. That era is over for me. But I want to say something. There are no words to describe how much I thank you. I will never forget you."

Blackie had meant a lot to me and had been a great role model. He had courage, dignity, toughness, and a certain sense of loving compassion for people who he respected. He had made working the pipelines a great experience for me and I had learned a lot from him.

"Remember your comment about the possibility of college. Are you going to leave Baton Rouge?"

I said, "I don't know. I may not be able to stay."

He got up from his seat, came over and shook my hand, and then he kissed me on the forehead. He looked at Nanny and then back at me. "You have greatness in you. I'll never forget you either. Keep on being yourself. You have everything it takes to succeed and you have the best teacher I've ever known." He was, of course, referring to Nanny whom he had known for a number of years and respected. Blackie then walked down the steps, got into his car, and left. I never saw him again.

Age: 19
Location: Baton Rouge,
Louisiana

22

## Decisions are tough...

Pipelines were over and I was back to some deep thinking about a lot of things as well as questions that I had no answers to. I needed a sounding board and Nanny smiled when I approached her about having some serious talks. "Have we had any other kind?" she asked.

Every morning found us together on the back porch, with the half-empty/half-full glass between us, talking about where I had come from, where I was going, what was everything about. What had I missed? What had I learned? The teachings I should have used but hadn't up until then.

I did know this much...I had come to the end of the road, tired of stealing, tired of serving time, tired of being arrested, tired of being questioned, tired of failing, and tired of being in a place where I could not keep from being treated as a criminal. In my mind, the answers seemed to be pointing in the direction of having to leave Baton Rouge, my beloved city, where I was born and raised and knew its every crook and cranny. The city had now become an emotional concrete solitary confinement. But the hardest part would be leaving my grandmother, which would be the equivalent of ripping my flesh off. She and my grandfather had stood behind me in complete and total support as they raised me as their fifth child. They were the only ones who I had been able to count on for the past 14 years as life had progressively become harder to handle.

But I knew things had to change.

If I had to leave, where would I go? How far would I go? What would my goal be?

The soul-searching and self-analysis continued for weeks with Nanny's help. Our discussion topics went from my early age of 2 ½ when I was studied at L.S.U., my father's aggression, being left by my mother at the age of seven, and progressed through to the time that I was sitting with her trying to make sense of all that had happened. To go from where I had been to setting a goal of a different future seemed impossible, but Nanny had been trying to teach me through the years to believe in the impossible, to never quit, be persistent, determined. That I had to have the faith of a Christ, Thoreau, Emerson, a Buddha, Edison, or Napoleon Hill; faith that the unseen would get you through whatever it is that you are trying to achieve.

My 19th birthday had come and gone and spring had replaced the winter months. I still occupied the back porch, having coffee and breakfast every morning and using the space for reading and making notations about the great achievers in the world. At one point, I made a list of about **ten great lessons that Nanny had taught**

**me** about life and made sure to tuck that list where I could pull it out when I needed it.

**10 Lessons of Life**
**The Law of Attraction (Change)**
*Being a positive person attracts positive people to want to be around you. Likewise, negative people are surrounded by negativity. Who is attracted to you is based on who you are and you have the ability to change accordingly.*

**The Law of the Universal Mind Within You**
*There is no greater power than the God within.*

**The Law of Self-Confidence and Self-Love**
*These are the tools that abolish doubt and fear.*

**Practice Concentration and Self-Control**
*Use the ability within you.*

**Copy the Habits of Great Achievers**
*Study their law of sacrificing lesser desires.*

**Believe in the Invisible**
*Have total faith in the Invisible operating within you.*

**Use Positive Affirmations**
*Master telling yourself who you are and who you are meant to be.*

**Praise What You Want Increased**
*Let God know what you need and how He can help you.*

**Aim High**
*Never give up. Have a purpose. Be single-minded. And remember you can do anything you want if you're willing to pay the price. Also remember, life is tough but you have to be tougher.*
**Like Thoreau Said, "Simplify Everything."**

I finally used one of our morning conversations to declare my thoughts out loud. "Nanny, I don't think I'll be able to make it here in Baton Rouge. I think I have to leave."

Nanny surprised me with her response. "I know. Your car is already packed. I could tell that's what you were going to do."

"How did you know?"

In her typical way, she smiled and put her hand on my arm. "I've been beside you since you were five. I know you as well as you know yourself, and you know that. I love you and I know that comes as no surprise to you either. Your car is packed. The money you have been saving is in your glove compartment. Do you know which direction you're going in?"

Decidedly, I said, "Texas. I've picked Fort Worth." There was a little nod of her head. "Not a bad pick."

Goodbyes were said and I was in the driver's seat before I had much time to think. Nanny gestured for me to roll down the window that she then leaned in through to give me some final thoughts to take with me. "This is it. I love you, but my suggestion is that you don't come back for at least a year and until you make something out of yourself, because you're either going to get killed or kill somebody, or they're going to put you in prison forever. This can't go on anymore."

I was able to say, "I know," but to honor her wishes was going to cut me in half. The tears started as soon as I left the driveway and did not stop until well past getting off the Huey P. Long Bridge on my way to Texas.

My immediate need was to make it to Fort Worth and find a job and an apartment, both of which took several days to accomplish, and my car became my living space until I could get settled. I felt very alone but found the nearest religious bookstore to follow up with what Nanny had suggested I do. "If you find yourself not able to be around me or have access to me, read the first four Gospels of the New Testament. Get Bibles where Jesus's words are in red and underline them. Keep a composition book with them in it and read them over and over again. Listen to what He's saying." I made notes and, over the next several months, read seven different versions of the four Gospels. I was finally putting action to some of the instructions Nanny had given. And it felt good.

An apartment and a job were found. The next goal was to work on school, a difficult one since I had not been able to finish the tenth grade. But I was supposed to believe in the impossible. I had, by invitation of the minister and his wife, spoken to a Baton Rouge church congregation. Parents wanted to know about my experiences, my suggestions for preventing the same thing from happening to the youth of their families. My readings of the Gospels had given me an idea and I called that minister to see if he had any suggestions for a Bible school near me in Fort Worth where I could learn more about what God had to teach me. He recommended Southwestern Seminary in Waxahachie, Texas, about 65 miles from where I lived and made an appointment for me there. From what he told me about the school, I was interested in knowing more, especially after he suggested that I should spend the summer there attending classes.

When I arrived on campus, I was met by a very kind and compassionate woman who, over lunch, asked me to tell her my story. She was obviously shocked by what I had to say. "Let me talk to the president of the college and see if we can get you to take the GED test today and qualify you for entrance."

My not finishing high school caused me to have great difficulty with the test...several times! After many attempts and much help from the woman I had met with, I finally passed! I took classes in 1961 and 1962 at the seminary, starting me down a much more positive road than I had previously traveled and causing other doors to open for me as well.

Age: 19
Location: Fort Worth,
Texas

# I had a plan...

I now had something positive to build on – a GED and having experienced classes in a secondary setting. These goals had been accomplished and succeeding had caused me to be hungry for more.

Nanny had always told me I 'knew people,' and that my readings of Sigmund Freud and Karen Horney, as well as others in the psychoanalysis and psychotherapy fields, had helped me to understand that everyone comes from a different background, some of which were odd, difficult and unknown. I guess from living in the streets, serving time in L.T.I., being in jail, reading great books by the hundreds, the one thing I could say was I knew something about people...what made them tick, what motivated them, what scared them, what changed them, how they had sacrificed, how many had lived like loners with no support but then had become some of life's greatest achievers. For better or for worse, I knew a lot about people. It's the only thing I could say that I really understood. That realization pointed me in a direction.

I had been noticing a woman each morning across the street from my apartment. She would sit on her front porch swing drinking her coffee and frequently observing me, but we had not yet had a conversation. She was out one morning and I crossed the street to make her acquaintance and, hopefully, get her opinion on some of the questions that I had been needing answers to recently. We made our introductions and one of the first questions I asked was, "Do you know how long it takes to become a psychotherapist?"

She thought a minute. "Well, you have to go to college for four years. Then it takes a couple of years to get a Master's Degree, so that's six. And then you may have to do some practicums or internships. So how old will you be if you spend six and a half years doing that? How old are you now?"

"I'm 19 years old. I would be…let's see, in six and a half years, 26 years old." I thanked her and started walking back across the street to my apartment.

She called out, "Young man?"

I turned around and said, "Yes, ma'am?"

"How old will you be in six and a half years if you don't become a psychotherapist?"

I stood in the street and looked at her. I said, "26, of course." I stood there for a moment before I said, "Thank you. Your point is well made."

After my conversation with my neighbor, I wanted more…more answers, more possibilities, more direction. Not knowing the first thing about how to make that happen, I approached a woman on the Texas Wesleyan College campus that was within walking distance of my apartment. She looked like she might work in some capacity at the school and I asked her who the boss of the school was. She looked me over pretty well and my appearance was not what it needed to be to make a good first impression. "I want to talk to the CEO or boss or whoever runs this place."

She said, "I'm awfully sorry. Most people go through the admissions office first, not Dr. Stone."

"Nevertheless, I'd like to speak to him."

Dr. Stone was walking into his office at that moment and overheard my conversation with his sec-

> "*Stand tall. Never give up. Greatness can only come from courage.*'"
>
> **Nanny**

retary, which prompted him to invite me into his office. Once I settled into one of the chairs, I said, "I'm looking forward to talking to you because I'd like to come to school here."

He offered coffee and he started asking me questions, prompting me to tell him about myself. When he found out that I hadn't gotten past the tenth grade, Dr. Stone was not encouraging. In fact, he said it was quite impossible for me to go to college, let alone to Texas Wesleyan, because of all of the teachings I had missed by not completing high school.

I was quick to respond, "I not only can give it a try, but I can also promise you without a shadow of a doubt that I'll be successful at it regardless of how much effort it takes on my part to succeed."

Our conversation continued for about an hour and a half and he was intrigued by the fact that my experience with literature had been so extensive.

There were more questions around my background in reading before he offered a possibility. "I'd like for you to meet and be seen by two people on our faculty."

The two people he picked were Dr. Dreger, head of the psychology department who had been psychoanalytically trained, and Dr. William Ward, a well-known writer. They both interviewed me for probably a couple of hours each. Dr. Dreger had me take a test during my time with him and asked me some questions about my past. I was guarded in what I shared based on my past experiences of people wanting to delve into my family relationships and how I had been affected by them. He heard about my street life, my living with my grandparents, and that I wanted to be a psychotherapist. I did confess that I had never been in counseling or therapy before but, if I was able to attend classes at Texas Wesleyan, I would want to build a relationship with him that would allow me to share more about my life.

Dr. Ward's time with me was spent in conversation at the end of which he pulled out one of his books and in the front of it wrote, "To a fellow writer," and signed it before handing it to me. I had never indicated to him that I was interested in writing and that this prediction had come from someone internationally known for his thoughts, ideas and writing was quite a surprise. But then again, this is being written in a book that you are reading, so he must have seen something in me that I wasn't aware of at the time.

Two days later, all four of us met in Dr. Stone's office and the comments made by both Dr. Ward and Dr. Dreger surprised me. Dr. Ward said, "This boy can do anything that he sets his mind to do. Not only is he determined, but he may also very well be the most well-read person of 19 years that I've ever met. He reads approximately 100 books a year and they're of the highest order. And he's obviously been raised by someone who is brilliant." Dr. Dreger seemed to be supportive of my attending the school as well, saying, "He is wise beyond his years. All he needs is a chance. I'm not only all for it, but in total agreement, and I would love to participate in this. I see this as an incredible experiment in human beings psychologically as well as our college."

It was Dr. Stone's turn to speak and he took a few minutes before turning to me. "How do you plan to address the teachings you missed in high school? Most of the college courses build on knowledge you don't have."

I had already thought about this. "There's a high school down the street and I will ask to borrow 10th, 11th and 12th-grade textbooks based on the courses I take.

That way I can use them as resources to keep up with the class assignments that I would be given."

He leaned back in his chair and looked at Dr. Dreger and Dr. Ward. "Was he like this when y'all interviewed him?"

They both said, "Absolutely."

Dr. Stone looked at me for a moment and then nodded. "I'll let you take three hours to get started and then come see me after this semester's over."

I asked one question before I left his office. "Would you write down the words psychotherapist and psycho-analysis for me so I know how they are spelled?" Dr. Dreger and Dr. Ward were smiling as Dr. Stone handed me what I had asked for.

*I was in!*

A few days later, I was standing in line for class registration, changed the "3" hours to "9" and proceeded to sign up for the courses listed on the girl's sheet who was standing in front of me. Before anyone could leave the registration area, you had to go through the fee line to pay for the classes you just signed up to take. Somebody standing close to me was talking about some huge amount—seven, eight hundred dollars or something. I had one penny in my pocket. When I reached the front of the line, I said, "My father will take care of this. Of all the things I have failed at, I can assure you that my father will take care of this in the right order. But if you want to go call the president, I'll wait in line." There were about 80 people behind me waiting in the hot sun in a line that stretched along the campus sidewalk.

The registrar hesitated but finally said, "Okay, okay, okay," allowing me to go through after stamping my paper. From there, I went to the bookstore and somehow was able to get the books I needed for my upcoming classes. Mr. Small, who ran the bookstore, and I wound up developing a great relationship during my time at Texas Wesleyan and I was allowed to bring in whatever money I could get to put against the balance I owed on my books. I was very grateful to him for working with me to make the books available for my use.

Some of the college classes I took were very challenging and I used the high school textbooks as references to give me the background I needed for the course studies. English was a nightmare because I had never learned how to dissect a sentence. The first assignment I turned in for my history class was an 80-page paper on George Fox and the development of the Quaker religion. I was called to the professor's office after handing in the assignment and worried on the way there that I must have done something wrong. His first question was had I been in college before. When I answered that I had not, he explained that the class assignment had only required a 2 to 3-page paper. To my surprise, he informed me that my work would keep me from having to take the midterm and final exams and he asked my permission to put my brief in the campus library. It was nice to have my efforts recognized.

I loved my courses in literature, most of which I took from Ms. Ruth Keating, who did her own form of therapy with me. I have a piece of paper from my time in her class that has written on it, I believe words by Goethe, that when you're capable of forgiving yourself for committing the most heinous crime that anyone else can commit then you will be able to forgive yourself and move on.

> *"Demand success. Be persistent. Aim high. Reach for the stars and sit with God."*
>
> **Nanny**

Later I spent three years in therapy with Dr. Dreger and spent years talking about the books and writing with Dr.William Ward, both of who were fantastic to me.

After the first semester, Dr. Stone said to proceed, and proceed I did. There was not much time for sleep. I continued my studies at the seminary through the first semester at Texas Wesleyan, which meant that I was attending classes on two different campuses for those few months. I consistently held down three jobs enabling me to get through college. I had copies of "The Dynamic Laws of Prosperity" by Catherine Ponder, "Franny and Zoey" by J.D. Sallinger, "Psychoanalysis" by Karen Horney, and "The Moon and Sixpence" by Somerset

Maugham. At least one of these books was with me every day probably for 15 years as I underlined parts of them to the point of having to put tape on the backs of all of them and finally having to resort to buying second, third and fourth copies as each wore out. I would read them at night and what I learned from those books got me through the tough times in college.

I worked hard, but it was satisfying. I focused everything that I had on learning all that this college had to teach. And I felt free.

Age: 19
Location: Fort Worth,
Texas

# 24

# Reflections on the impossible...

The day I registered for classes is one that has stood out in my mind ever since. I left the campus knowing what my course load would be, excited to get it started, and walked a couple of blocks to an open park where I found a large tree to sit against. It was beginning to sink in that my future was not going to be behind bars; rather it would be one of my own choosing and that I had started taking the steps needed to accomplish the impossible. That I was living up to what Nanny told me I could do.

My grandmother had said something confusing—"I can get you to heaven's gate. I just can't get you past it." I didn't know what that meant when she had said it and she had said those words more than once.

At the time that I lost my father, my mother leaving me, when I was living on the streets, arrested dozens of times, challenging authority figures to end up in a place where children were despised, harmed—that didn't feel like heaven, It didn't look like heaven either. The only thing that was left if I had stayed was more suffering. And that realization had turned me in another direction.

I now wanted the opposite. I wanted a place to learn, a place where I would understand things, a place to grow. And I finally felt that freedom knew my name!

*"Real winning IS A LONG TRAIN TO HEAVEN. But, if you never give up, you arrive at the Golden Gate."*

**Nanny**

It flowed through me as I was sitting there—I finally understood Nanny's wisdom. Getting through heaven's gate is only something you can do for yourself. People can help you get to the gate, but the actual opening of it is not within their ability. It's something you have to want for yourself—from inside your mind and heart. While it may be hard to get to heaven's gate, the universal mind behind it is waiting to welcome you. All you have to do is use one finger, or use the breath from one affirmation and the gate will open. But it's a universal law that you are the only one who can do it for yourself.

I felt like I had just opened heaven's gate. It was within me to do that and the discovery of that was overwhelming. It's invisible. It's the other half of a glass of water that Nanny always set out to teach me about life. There was substance and there was the invisible. The invisible requires faith—something that I had finally acquired.

Age: 24
Location: Baton Rouge,
Louisiana

# 25

# 1966 with Judge Pugh...

It seemed like lifetimes ago that my encounters with the law and courts had happened, yet I was now seeking out another judge, this time to see if he could help me. I had completed the first year of Clinical Psychology at the University of North Texas but I was finding that my past actions and my record were causing problems for my present and limitations for my future. I had made inquiries about expungement and those brought me to Judge Pugh's office in downtown Baton Rouge. I was hoping he would have some answers.

The judge's assistant, named Jeannette, was able to locate my files after I told her what I was wanting. She returned to her office with two files, one for my juvenile record, the other for my adult record. "Don't I know your uncle and your mother? I think I do. Let me talk to the judge. You wait here." She came back to her desk after a few minutes and took the two file folders back into his office with her.

Judge Pugh called out from behind his desk, "Come in and have a seat."

I settled into the chair in front of his desk, not knowing how much of the judge's time I would be allowed to have. But I needed some answers and I was looking for direction of where to go next to, hopefully, make my past mistakes stop haunting me.

The judge was leafing through my files on the desk as he spoke. "I have court this morning, I can meet with you around…" and he stopped talking. A few moments of concentration on one of the documents in front of him and then he looked at me. "I remember now. You're Darryl Wheat. Two professors have called and written to me about you, that I should be expecting to see you someday, and here you are. You're currently in college and halfway through a Master's Degree in Psychology, is that correct?"

I answered, "Yes…yes, Your Honor."

The judge's focus went back to my record and I watched his facial expressions change as he read slowly. There were times when he would look up from the pages he had been studying, obviously thinking.

"Jeannette," he called from behind his desk. When she appeared in the doorway, "Announce that court will be postponed 30 minutes, starting at 9:30 this morning." She disappeared again and the judge went back to studying the files.

He continued to study the file documents. "How many times do you think that you were arrested? The list just goes on for pages and pages throughout this folder.

How many times do you think you were arrested?"

I said, "Probably around 40 times that I was picked up." "And how many charges?"

I answered, "Probably around 30 or 40. I don't know."

"I can see what

*Official charges on the record:*
*Theft (multiple)*
*Shoplifting (multiple)*
*Selling stolen goods (multiple)*
*Vehicle theft (3 including 1 speed boat)*
*Assault (multiple)*
*Burglary – business (multiple)*
*Burglary – car (multiple)*
*Burglary – train*
*Aggravated battery (multiple)*
*Jail escapes (multiple)*

they're for. A lot of jail escapes. The number of jails you've been in—New Orleans, Baton Rouge, Alexandria, Monroe, New Roads, Appaloosas, Mississippi, Alabama. These arrests. How many escapes?"

"I think there were 12," I said.

"How many sentences?" His focus went back to the files. "It looks to me like there were four sentences, not counting the ones for probation and for parole after you got out. How many times were you in solitary?"

"I think I was in solitary around six or seven times but in different places."

"Jeannette? Help me count this stuff, but tell everybody that court will now start at 10:00. "

Judge Pugh pulled a letter from his desk. A little more reading was followed by more questions. "Is this true that you never finished the tenth grade? You've gotten a Bachelor's Degree in Psychology and you're halfway through with a Master's Degree in Clinical Psychology? And you've already been through the testing and the practicums and internship and then you will be a psychotherapist and a psychologist, from what I understand. According to one of your professors, this is what you wrote down that you wanted to be. Is that true?"

"Yes, Your Honor, that is true."

Judge Pugh leaned back in his chair and all focus was put on me. "This seems to be almost impossible...in fact, almost a miracle. Certainly unbelievable." After a few moments, he said, "I would like for you to go into the courtroom with me and let me tell the people there how this happened and a few things that I want to say. Will you do this for me?"

"Yes, sir."

We walked into the court and he took his seat. I was one of about 50 or 60 people who were in attendance to hear what he had to say. Judge Pugh directed his comments to the whole room and started down the list: the number of times I was arrested, sentenced, in solitary confinement, dozens and dozens and dozens of fistfights. He told everyone that I had been shot, stabbed, hit in the face that caused 90 stitches and required three operations to repair. He continued to tell my story of being put on probation at the age of 13, incarcerated for about a year at 14, on parole from 15 to 18 and violated parole approximately 12 times. He finished telling about my past with a statement of my present—that I was currently halfway through my Master's Degree on my way to becoming a psychotherapist, but that I was able to do so because I had changed.

"This is what I want you people who are sitting here to understand—that life can be different and that you don't always have to be in trouble. This young man changed his mood. He changed his actions. He changed his life. He changed his commitment to what he wanted to be. In front of you present in this courtroom, I am now going to sign an expungement of his juvenile and adult records."

His next comments were directed to me. "Mr. Wheat, before hearing the problems of the day before me in this court, it is my privilege to personally expunge the longest juvenile record I have ever seen in my career, and your adult record as well. This court is proud of you. You have seemingly accomplished the impossible both personally and educationally. We both expect and look forward to, with great appreciation, your future accomplishments, and your personal and professional contributions. The court will now take a ten-minute break."

Judge Pugh escorted me back to his office area where he had me sit in his waiting room. I could hear him making a phone call and it was to my uncle. "P.V., I just expunged your nephew's five-pound file folder. He has accomplished a miracle."

There were a few minutes of silence while my uncle was obviously responding to the news on the other end of the conversation. P.V. later let me know that he had greeted the news with pride and tears.

The judge reappeared at his doorway shortly after hanging up the phone. "If you ever need anything, call me. I'll buy the coffee." He smiled and hugged me. Jeannette walked over and hugged me. He said, "I have to go. I have people to teach who haven't yet learned what you've learned. So, take care, son."

"Yes, sir."

I walked out of the judge's office, crossed the street to North Boulevard. I was back in my beloved Baton Rouge, and free. In front of me was Third Street and the newsstand. I took a left past the beautiful old state capital and past Second Street. I walked down to the levee near the old rusty railroad tracks.

I remembered the ferry that went back and forth across the river to Port Allen. To my right was the old bridge. To my left was the new one. I had grown up with the Mississippi River; the tugboats, the barges, the workmen along the river. I had lived with the river and I had taken it for granted, even though I had crossed it throughout my life. This day, I was sitting on the levee free. It brought pieces of my life back to me. I loved sitting there next to this old, great river. I felt completely back home again.

After a minute, I pulled out the piece of paper from my pocket that I had purposely put there that morning. It was a worn piece of tablet paper on which Nanny had written the words "Isn't life wonderful?"

*"...what you believe in, aspire to...you will one day become. Your dream is merely the Universal Mind's (God's) promise to you regarding what you are capable of achieving. Accept the responsibility of your dream and reap the benefits of your vision.*

**Nanny**

*Before leaving Baton Rouge, I had made up my mind that I would change my entire life. No one would know me. I could start over and make something of me. I had read enough about great people to know what they did that was wholesome, honest, spiritual and successful, and my goal was to apply what others had said and done and follow their lead. It didn't mean giving up my personality – just my way of life AND changing my attitude. I also needed to reframe the word 'failure' so that it became a series of errors supplemented by changes and successes.*

**Dr. Darryl Wheat**

## Personal Achievements

### Degrees

- Texas Wesleyan University - B.A. in Psychology
- University of North Texas - M.S. in Clinical Psychology
- Universal Academy of Truth - Ph.D. in Metaphysical Religion
- Louisiana State University - M.S.W. in Clinical Social Work – Board-Certified Diplomat
- Smith College - Ph.D. in Clinical Social Work (Psychoanalytic Theory with Psychodynamic Emphasis on Trauma in Children in Early Childhood and Adults)

- University of Mississippi Medical Center – Three-year study under Dr. Edgar Draper, Director of Clinical Psychiatry and Psychoanalysis to become Board-Certified Diplomat

## Other Educational Experiences

- Assembly of God University - one year of Religious Studies
- University of Oklahoma - one year studying Child Psychology
- University of Pennsylvania - Dean's Merit and Scholarship Award for Special Studies in clinical Social Work and Mental Health
- Meninger Clinic, Topeka, KS - special training sessions
- Special training from Dr. Peter Giovacinni, psychoanalyst, regarding the theories of Dr. Donald Winnecott, psychoanalyst

## Notable Experiences

Under Fulton County Mental Health of Atlanta, GA:
- 4½ years as Clinical Director teaching Psychotherapy in four mental health centers, four mentally-handicapped children's centers and the Atlanta Drug Abuse Program
- Reported weekly progress, meetings and problems to then-Governor Jimmy Carter (future

president of the United States) under the Director of Fulton County Mental Health
- Conducted lectures to keep Georgia residents informed of the state's mental health needs. Notable attendees were Governor Jimmy Carter, Coretta Scott King and Congressmen Julian Bond, United Nations Ambassador Andrew Young, and Mayor Maynard Jackson

## Notable Consultations With:

- Ed Draper
- Albert Ellis
- Erik Erikson
- Viktor Frankl
- Peter Giovacinni
- Rollo May
- Meninger Clinic (Staff Members)
- Gerald Patterson
- Fritz Pearls
- Martin Seligman
- B.F. Skinner
- Joseph Wolpe
- Irving Yallom

## Notable Experiences and Accomplishments (Spiritual) With:

Ernest Holmes, Joseph Murphy, Catherine Ponder, Roy Eugene Davis, Jack Addington, David Schwartz, Susan Jeffers

## Professional Highlights

- Counseled over 25,000 clients in therapy
- Counseled over 500 children in therapy for sexual abuse
- Delivered approximately 300 workshops in seven states
- Trained over 50 people in Psychotherapy
- Consulted with or given professional assistance to approximately 1,000 psychotherapists
- Written three books
- Published in professional journals

## Dr. Darryl Wheat currently practices under the following licenses and specialties:

- Licensed and Board-Certified Clinical Social Worker
- Psychoanalyst (Board-Certified Diplomat)

- Specialty: Children and adults who have experienced traumatic childhood and young adult experiences, including sexual abuse
- Forensic Court Expert, having testified in over 600 cases in 7 states

*"One day you will become great. You will become a model for others, you will succeed, and you will conquer. It's your destiny. The Infinite already knows it's your destiny. Stand tall."*

**Nanny**

# Insights Into The Author

**Q: Why was it so important for you to write "The Greatest Comeback?"**

**A:** I have at least 20 other books I would have found easier to write. I wrote this book because I owe my Creator a book that teaches people not to abandon their dreams and to never give up. I feel that I would be less than honest if I hadn't shared with children, parents and professionals some of the life lessons that I had to learn the hard way—that you can change, succeed and love others and your own life with much less support from your environment. In other words, I wanted them to know that "they can make it" and nothing really can stop them once putting their mind to it.

I wanted to share my grandmother with the world, my Nanny. The strength she had and the intelligence she shared in her support of me and what I went through was nothing short of amazing. She was inspirational to me and, if she could influence others through this book, then this book has accomplished all that I wanted it to. I promised her that I would write my story.

This book was not written to correct the penal system. It was written to educate others about the experiences that a youth went through—me. If that can change the direction in one life…if a parent can help a child avoid the narcissism and hate of the correctional institutions… then the time and the effort of writing this book has been worth it.

I wanted people who had been in L.T.I. and other correctional facilities to know that I, as well as they, can change and succeed regardless of their past circumstances.

## Q: What do you want the readers to take from reading this book?

**A:** The knowledge that no circumstances can prevent you from succeeding. Success comes from your mind. It's mental. It has nothing to do with external circumstances. You can create your own circumstances.

## Q: Why did you wait so long to write this book?

**A:** Each member of my core family encouraged me to, at some point, write this book. My mother, when she was dying, asked me to please write my story. I waited and put it off probably because of the pain it would cause.

Very few people knew the reality of all that I went through in my youth. I knew in writing the book that I would start reliving some of my past experiences. What I didn't know is that making the decision to start the book would cause the startup of nightmares, insomnia, visualizations of certain events. That was before I actually sat down to write it. I have experienced all of those traumas through the year it has taken to finish "Comeback."

**Q: You experienced more difficulty and emotion toward the end of writing the book. Why?**

**A:** Because it brings up some of the most painful things you can experience. The good thing about it is that you finally get it out of your system.

This book has been in my future for over 40 years. I anticipated it and created it in my mind long before I ever put anything down on paper. By finishing it, that process will be over. And in a lot of ways, by finishing it I will be saying another goodbye to Nanny, my mother and some other family members who saw my struggles.

**Q: For much of your youth, you disrespected the law. Did you think that you should not be in trouble for some of the things that you did?**

**A:** My thoughts didn't center on those kinds of questions. The whole story started slowly by my family breaking up and us moving to my grandmother's. I started taking up for myself and it just grew. My thoughts were more on 'I don't care,' self-protection and survival.

**Q: How would you change the penal system for youth?**

**A:** You said half of it – you take away the 'penal' part of it. What is necessary is to train, teach, support, educate, and, above all, immerse the children in psychotherapy with loving, caring people. Or provide them with mentors or a surrogate family. Change doesn't come from a meeting. It comes from the freedom and effort to try to succeed, be loved, and be cared for.

Treat the individual rather than the mass. Treating the whole 450 children as a group, as they did at L.T.I., to line up, be fed, to be whipped is to skillfully avoid individual children. They needed to work with 450 individuals in trying to live a loving and productive life. There should be no reform schools. There should be therapeutic centers. I plan to write about this in one of my next books. If you want a child to be a healthy citizen, you build it to be a therapy center. If you want the child to be a criminal, make it a penal system. If it's not changed, you're just creating more criminals each year. You're not creating mentally healthy, adaptive, productive children. The system should be preventive and proactive versus reactive.

## Q: What is your advice for parents who read this book?

A: Underline the things you think are important to improve your relationship with your child. If you're going to read the book, try to understand deeply that, if your child is in trouble, you're going to have to make some serious decisions about what's going to happen with your child. Give some thought to your own behavior. Have the child read this book or read it to them.

## Q: What is your advice for youth who read this book?

**A:** Believe what you're reading. Do you really want to suffer the consequences? Do you really want to suffer the consequences that are expressed in this book? If you're old enough, try to have some insight into where you're headed in life. What do you want? What do you want life to be?

## Q: What groups have you spoken to about your experiences? Are there others you think would benefit from hearing about your experiences?

**A:** Schools, correctional facilities, professional therapists, psychiatrists, extended families, the medical profession (particularly nurses), police.

Incidentally, all churches should have a speaker regarding this and bring the children to the event. Also, I highly recommend, and would be willing to consider, communicating with ministers, priests, and other religious representatives regarding work with troubled children and children who have already gotten into serious legal trouble.

## Q: There were people throughout your life who have heard your story and been wanting you to write a book. Who were some of these people?

**A:** President Jimmy Carter; Coretta Scott King; the authors of "Chicken Soup For The Soul"; numerous college and graduate school professors and deans; Dr. Stone, President of Texas Wesleyan University; numerous judges including Judge Pugh of Baton Rouge, LA; Susan Jeffers who wrote "Feel The Fear And Do It Anyway"; the family of Dr. Joseph Murphy (renowned author); Catherine Ponder (world-renowned minister and author); Robert Collier; Orison Marden.

But the most important group that has supported the writing of this book is made up of the individuals who shared my experience at the Louisiana Training Institute. They wanted it known what they experienced behind the barbed wire fences.

# Suggested Reads

*My life has been directly influenced by books by and about great people. The list below includes selections of self-help and biographies that I would recommend as a starting point for great reading. Self-help books are self-explanatory but I found that the biographies of great people that I have read have the same things in common – the strong will persevere and change themselves and the world around them no matter what the circumstances. Enjoy!*

**Dr. Darryl Wheat**

- The Perfect Power Within You – Jack Addington
- As A Man Thinketh – James Allen
- Key to Yourself – Venice Bloodworth
- Secret of the Ages – Robert Collier
- Think and Grow Rich – Napoleon Hill
- The Hidden Secret – Christian Larson
- How to Get What You Want – Orison Marden
- The Moon and Sixpence – Somerset Maugham
- The Dynamic Laws of Prosperity – Catherine Ponder
- Franny and Zooey – J. D. Sallinger

- Walden – Henry David Thoreau
- The Science of Being Great – Wallace Waddles
- The Genius of Great Achievers – Dr. Darryl Wheat

# Favorite Quotes

*Individuals have influenced me. I daily carry a tablet filled with my favorite quotes as well as books that are just about worn through because of all of the underlines throughout and the dog-eared-ness of the pages. I have included some of my favorites hoping that you will find some of the motivation and inspiration in them that I have.*

**Dr. Darryl Wheat**

## Henry David Thoreau:

"I learned this, at least by my experiment: that if one advances confidently in the direction of his dreams, and endeavors to live the life which he had imagined, he will meet with a success unexpected in common hours."

STOP      STOP      STOP      STOP

*(Human beings typically fail to mention the second part of this quote. Thousands of self-help books quote the above portion. Millions need to learn about the second half, which has been added below. The second half explains our relationship with Infinite Intelligence and the spiritual life consequences of finding the God within us, what He does for us, how we have been reinvented, and the greatness that's been bestowed upon us when we go inside and find our true selves.)*

## BUT THE IMPORTANT PART IS:

"He will put some things behind, will pass an invisible boundary; new, universal, and more liberal laws will begin to establish themselves around and within him; or the old laws expanded, and interpreted in his favor in a more liberal sense, and he will live with the license of a higher order of beings."

### Sigmund Freud:

"The crumbs of knowledge offered in these pages, though they have been laboriously enough collected, may not in themselves prove very satisfying; but they may serve as a starting for the work of investigators and common endeavor may bring the success which is perhaps beyond the reach of individual effort."

### Christian Larson:

"Faith is the hidden secret to greatness because faith takes man into the inner life of that power that produces greatness. Therefore, he who has faith in himself may become anything, attain anything and accomplish anything."

### Bruce Barton:

"Nothing splendid has ever been achieved except by those who dared believe that something inside of them was superior to their circumstance."

**Napoleon Hill:**

"Through some strange and powerful principal of mental 'chemistry' which she has never divulged, nature wraps up in the impulse of strong desire, that 'something' which recognizes no such word as 'impossible,' and accepts no such reality as failure."

**Napoleon Hill:**

"Effort only fully releases its reward after a person refuses to quit."

**Napoleon Hill:**

"I realize the dominating thoughts of my mind will eventually reproduce themselves in outward, physical action, and gradually transform themselves into a physical reality."

# About the Author

Dr. Darryl Wheat is a widely known psychotherapist, inspirational speaker, personal achievement consultant, frequent trainer in Spiritual and Success Psychology, and author of several books. He is engaged in frequent seminars, workshops and public speaking. He is particularly called on to speak to college audiences, churches, retreats, business clubs, and organizations.

He currently maintains a private practice in Mississippi. He is well-known for his expertise with traumatized children and divorce. He is widely used as an expert witness.

He has a B.S. degree from Texas Wesleyan University, and M.S. degree from University of North Texas, a M.S.W. from Louisiana State University, has been a scholarship student at the University of Pennsylvania, has Ph.D. in Religion, and a Ph.D. in Clinical Social Work from Smith College. He also completed Psychoanalytic Training and is a Board-Certified Psychoanalyst.

To contact Dr. Darryl Wheat for speaking engagements, lectures:

Dr. Darryl Wheat
Cell: 601-613-5250
d-wheat@hotmail.com

www.ingramcontent.com/pod-product-compliance
Lightning Source LLC
Chambersburg PA
CBHW061143120626
46546CB00005B/1901